Goddess Lessons

Discover the Wisdom and Strength of the Divine Feminine

LAURIE SUE BROCKWAY

Goddess Lessons

Digital Edition 2019
Publisher: Goddess Communications, LLC
Cover Design and Interior Formatting: Qamber Designs & Media
Editor: June Soyka Cook of Self-Healing Expressions
Proofreading: Proofing With Style
All Images used under license from: Shutterstock.com and DepositPhotos.com
Additional research provided by: Rev. Dr. Victor Fuhrman, D.Scd, MSC, RM
Lessons 5, 7, 9, 11, and 13 adapted from: The Goddess Pages, ©Laurie Sue Brockway

Apologies to the Goddess in advance for any errors in presenting Her history, information, prayers, and rituals.

ISBN-10: 194163017
ISBN-13: 978-1-941630-17-4

Contents

Introduction

HOW I DISCOVERED THE PATH OF THE GODDESS

"Never instead of, always in addition to."
— Rabbi Joseph Gelberman

"The simplest and most basic meaning of the symbol of the Goddess is the acknowledgment of the legitimacy of female power as a beneficent and independent power."
— Carol P. Christ

WHILE DEEP INTO THE STUDY of comparative religions in seminary school I was surprised to discover that there were many feminine faces of the Divine. There are literally thousands of goddesses, from many of the world's cultures, known by different names and images, which represent feminine aspects of divinity and also aspects of our humanity. The Hindu, Buddhist, Tibetan, Native American, and South American cultures are among the traditions that continue to commune with the Divine Feminine.

I found God in feminine form and she looked like me. I especially grew attached to the Hindu Goddess Lakshmi. It changed my life to know there was a feminine component to the male God I grew up with.

Over twenty years ago I set out on a mission: to let people know that the concept of the goddess is not a made-up thing, that goddesses have been worshipped for eons, from the very start of creation. I believe that the Goddess was intentionally dropped out of many holy books and teachings; over time, honoring of women was also dropped out. That's why women sometimes feel disenfranchised from their own faith; or disconnected from their own divinity.

We've been raised in a culture that's given us millions of images of the male divine, and ideas of the male divine, and the language of the male divine, without giving us a language and a vocabulary for a feminine divine. So, on the deepest cellular level of our beings, women feel like they're not included in divinity. And this also excludes them from feeling powerful.

I have found over time many women feel empowered by seeing themselves as a living link to the Divine Feminine. It can greatly enhance self-esteem and spirituality.

This book began as a course called Discovering the Goddess and I have left it in the form of lessons to help you learn more about goddess history and to offer rituals and prayers to help you connect to the Goddess.

You don't have to replace the male divine with the feminine. I would argue that they stand side by side in religious history and should stand side by side in modern worship. Not all religions would agree.

The Goddess Path is different from other paths and you are free to create your own interpretation and a personal divine relationship. Many people feel more connected to a greater force when they personify the divine. For some people, it's more comfortable viewing the Goddess in this way:

- Archetype or messenger
- Gender-neutral force or being
- Non-religious or nondenominational power source
- Non-descriptive higher power
- Special energy or feeling
- Divine beings with names and faces
- An aspect of spirit that cannot be defined or labeled

Many people yearn to know more, yet grapple with the idea of goddess because they've been taught there is no goddess–

there's only God. I believe you can have both if you choose to.

Ultimately, everyone must find their own path. These lessons are designed to provide an overview of goddess history and goddess spirituality to those who seek more insight. They are designed to show a mix of different interpretations of the Goddess and ways she's been worshipped around the world.

I hope that women who are called to the Goddess will find that stepping onto the path makes them happier and allows them to accept themselves for who they are. Goddess spirituality can help them get to the core of their being, their inner soul, their inner goddess.

What I love about including the Goddess in our view and experience of divinity is that she is a spiritual mother. Just as our mothers give us life the divine mother can bring a deeper connection to all of creation. The Divine Feminine can complement any spiritual practice because she brings balance.

You may experience the Divine Feminine as a living and breathing goddess and be blessed to have such a full experience with her. In these pages you will find ways to feel that energy all around you and develop a connection to God, Goddess, to all that is.

Many thanks!

Rev. Laurie Sue

Lesson One

WELCOME

"One person's mythology is another person's religion."
— Joseph Campbell

WELCOME TO THE WORLD OF THE GODDESS!

You are about to embark on a spiritual journey of learning about the Divine Feminine and how she can help you in daily life.

Goddess history dates back to the earliest civilizations. It's well documented that ancient societies worshiped feminine forms of God—typically as mother, earth, and nature, or as deities who personified feminine attributes. Theologians, archeologists, historians, and experts in religious mythology have told of literally thousands of goddesses from cultures around the world.

Worship of the Divine Mother permeated ancient societies. Her temples abounded. Her presence was expressed in the images, and stories that were passed along through countless generations. Many of the world's cultures continue to worship, honor, and pray to female deities. The Hindu, Buddhist, Tibetan, Native American, South American, and African cultures are among those that always have, and continue to, commune with the Divine Feminine. Today, she is also actively honored as earth, and by countless ancient names, by practitioners of modern goddess spirituality.

She is known by many names and faces, from many traditions and cultures, but she does not ask you to give up the faith you were born into or the spiritual beliefs you cherish. Rather, she comes into your life in addition to any other form of spirituality you hold dear, to enhance who you already are and open a new way for you to see and know yourself; and to help you find a firmer footing on your spiritual path.

In the upcoming lessons, you will discover the Goddess and how her special wisdom and power can help heal, inspire and uplift you, your relationships, and the world. You will also be guided to connect to the divinity within and to claim your sacred feminine power and your connection to the Goddess. If you have been earnestly searching for Her, this course will help you onto the path.

ON THIS INSPIRING AND HEALING JOURNEY, YOU WILL...

- Explore the history of the Goddess.
- Learn about the cultures and traditions that honor Her today.
- Meet Her in her many forms, and by her many names.
- Have a chance to practice healing rituals and exercises that can help you in all areas of life.
- Receive special blessings, insights, and knowledge.
- Enter the sacred circle of Her love and protection to meditate and plan your life's dreams.
- And when you are ready, step into the inner Temple of the Goddess to connect deeply with Her through your heart, soul, and prayer.

You are encouraged to give deep thought to the new things you discover and to do more research on your own. This book may be a stepping stone to the diverse world of the Goddess and many other writings on this topic. Open your heart and mind as fully as possible, to a new way of seeing God—with a feminine face, attributes and attitude—and to a new way of experiencing spirituality.

WHO KNEW THERE WAS A GODDESS?

Most women were not exactly raised to believe that within us is a divine power that is feminine in nature. Most of us were taught that divinity is male. And that it is found in men, in churches, and through clergy people. When we were growing up, we were more likely playing with princess dolls than chatting about drawing inspiration from divine female role models who looked like us. When upset about something, brokenhearted or confused, it is unlikely anyone around your house suggested, "Go within, or connect with the Goddess."

Many of us have come to know "Goddess" as the title bestowed on 1950s divas of the screen or as women and celebrities who embody an astounding physical beauty that most of us could never hope to emulate. Yet some of us recall our earliest experience with goddesses in high school social studies, where we studied mythology. Even though some of the classical Greek and Roman mythology painted divine women as conniving—and even a bit masculine—in their approach, the tales of Titan beings with superpowers gave us our first glimpse of Divine Feminine power: The independent Artemis. The brilliant war strategist Athena. The harbinger of victory Nike. The seductive and alluring Venus. Without us even giving it much thought, they have all been integrated into our culture, and accepted as symbols of female prowess—cool women who make up their own rules!

PERMISSION TO BE ALL WE CAN BE

Many modern women, in all age ranges, want to learn how to make up their own rules and confidently follow the call of their hearts. Many dream of creating lives of their own making and living them joyously, without apology. Many seek healing from old beliefs, heartaches, and current maladies. There are many awesome archetypes that look like us and have traits we may want to emulate—and stories that we, as women, can relate to. I believe that the mere concept of female divinity gives us mortal women permission to be all we can be. It makes practical sense to identify our own goddess nature, and our connection to the Divine Feminine, and consciously strengthen it.

Without even realizing it, many of us stumble onto the Goddess the same way we find God—during a time of crisis, great need or pain, or during moments of extraordinary passion, and full participation in life. We find Her when we call upon the great reserve of power that lies within us to get through a tough experience. We discover Her when we find love and feel love and walk around openhearted and happy. We come across Her in the course of trying to make ourselves stronger, fitter, happier, and more successful in life. We hear Her voice when we meditate or seek deeper wisdom. It's just that we have not been taught, for the most part, to consciously evoke Her, connect to Her, and pray to Her.

Most of us have been raised with an understanding of a male God, with little insight into the existence of the Goddess or the feminine aspects of aspects of God. However, if you deeply study all the world's religions you will find that even the most male-dominated traditions have holy references to the softer, gentler, more forgiving and feminine aspects of the male God. However, gentleness is not the only trait assigned to the feminine divine. Many cultures have goddesses who are also wild and unpredictable in nature and they often have consorts who match or balance their energy. In this course, we will take a very interfaith approach to the Divine Feminine and will meet and explore diverse goddesses from different traditions.

THE DIVINE WITHIN US ALL

Let's begin our studies together by considering the premise that the light of the Divine lives within us and that we all—male and female—are connected to God and Goddess. And that aspects of both feminine and masculine exist in us all. Some people will relate more to divinity as a gender-neutral energy or force and that is also a wonderful way to view the Divine. When I pray I like to use the term "God, Goddess, All there is" so that everyone is covered.

We all begin our lives as divine beings, our souls brought onto this earth from no less a place than the heavens. Thus, in my opinion, we are all divine in nature. It's just that we sometimes forget. Now is the time to remember. None of us can expect to connect to the true source of our power until we understand that we are truly made in the image of the divine, created in the image of a Creator who must look like us, if we look like Her! At the very least, let us entertain the idea that just as we come into this world in the image of and with the characteristics of our human parents, we are also blessed with the same from our divine parents.

Men have always been raised with images and pictures of divinity that have instilled confidence in them and made them feel connected to God and have made them feel and act like gods. And women just have not had that advantage. We have to create it, now.

SHE IS RE-EMERGING

There was a time in history when God WAS a woman. And then a point in history when she at least sat on her own throne, right next to the Divine Father. Throughout history, she has been there, but the telling of Her story has been adapted, and altered. For about two thousand years it seemed she was dropped from scriptures and religious studies, and eventually, our consciousness. Our Christian-Judaic-Islamic based culture for a long time dominated our view of religion, and still does. But research in modern times has shown that the Goddess has been actively worshiped by other religions for centuries and was the primary deity millennia ago. Wicca is one of the earth-based tradition focused on the worship of the Divine Female as the main deity and it is a spiritual practice that continues to grow and become more a part of the mainstream. Beyond the goddess-based religions, there are many schools of spiritual study today that espouse the Feminine Divine as a primary deity.

The Goddess is re-emerging now to show us another side of ourselves. Or at least to help us consider God is both masculine and feminine in nature. And she's come just in time. We need her back in our consciousness and back in our world!

Anyone who has ever experienced divorce or separation in their family life knows how difficult it is to find balance when Dad lives in one place, and Mom lives in another—and how the kids feel forced to choose loyalty to one or the other. I think the same holds true for our divine parents. Why should any of us, ever, under any circumstances, feel forced to choose one over the other?

WHAT WOULD HAPPEN IF…

We simply trusted that they are always there for us and that we could easily call upon them both? That the most appropriate spiritual energy is available at the appropriate time? That men and women can express both masculine and feminine energy and experience the feminine and masculine aspects of God. Having one doesn't mean giving up the other.

We need the special energies of the Divine Mother more than ever because:

Women, increasingly, feel left out of traditional religion. It's not just about becoming a clergy person or having political power, it's about being able to recognize our own divinity. Men have been able to recognize their divinity through worship of a male divine. It's time that women access the Goddess within. And that we feel honored by a spirituality that speaks to us and for us.

Men are shut off from their feminine energy and, quite frankly, their softness in many cases. There is so little in religious environments and in our culture—and most of the world's traditions and cultures—that nurtures that side of males. Because of this, men are suffering, women and children are suffering, and our world is suffering—big time!

Because of the ingrained idea of a male divinity, our relationship lives are utterly confusing. Love, for many, means war. Instead of accessing all the qualities of the male and feminine in ourselves, we seek partners to make us whole. We have to learn to come into relationships whole and we can only do that when we embrace all aspects of ourselves and the divine.

We've got kids to raise, and it's time we teach them that ALL OF WHO THEY ARE IS OKAY. That their sex doesn't have to assign them to specific gender roles. That we are all made up of the male and female principle, the yin and the yang–or that they don't have to be assigned gender roles at all. (But for the purpose of this book we are looking at the inclusion of the feminine and masculine principle). If we raise our boys to know the divine only in male terms then we deny them access to a part of themselves. And if we teach our girls that the feminine divine only exists in fairy tales, they will grow up missing the opportunity to feel like—and be—goddesses in human form.

WE LIVE IN A WORLD SPINNING OUT OF CONTROL

We are at war with one another and within ourselves. I won't even go into the politics of our time. Suffice to say our world is in trouble.

Could it be because we have mistreated our great mother—Mother Earth—and Mom Nature is trying to get our attention? As it is said in the old Lakota Chant, "The earth is our mother, we must take care of her."

In these pages, you will learn more about how to connect with the Goddess in various ways.

GETTING ORGANIZED FOR THIS COURSE

Lessons often build on previous lessons and for this reason it is suggested that you create a file or have a place to keep all your notes, thoughts, and assignments. This will provide you with a way to create a sacred container for your goddess work.

1. **Start A Goddess Journal**
   Designate a notebook or journal as your "Goddess Journal," to use for notes and exercises we will be doing in this course.
2. **Set Your Intentions for this Course**
   The first thing you could write in your journal is your intention for this course. As part of your intentions, you could literally invite the goddesses to make their presence known to you (a symbol or synchronicity, perhaps?) throughout this course, and beyond. Once you have composed your intention, say it aloud and meditate on it for a few moments.
3. **Mother's Embrace Meditation**
   Take a shower, put on fresh clothing, and sit in a quiet place where you can allow your heart and mind to open in gentle meditation. Light a candle if possible to illuminate the moment with a symbol of divine light.

Imagine your mother's or grandmother's house (or the nurturing female in your own life). Feel that feeling of warmth and welcome; connect to a place that always feels like home.

Now imagine that your Divine Mother has a special place as well. It is not a physical place, rather, a place that dwells within you. When you are with her there you feel safe, protected and warm; you feel well-fed and filled up with spirit.

Feel what it is like in Mother's embrace and know that your Divine Mother offers you that kind of love and more.

Write down the qualities you experienced in the above meditation in your Goddess Journal.

CLOSING THOUGHTS

It is time to create wholeness within ourselves. But to put it simply, it is time to listen to our Divine Mother. See if she speaks to you, shows you images or shares wisdom with you in daily life.

NEXT LESSON

Where Has She Been?

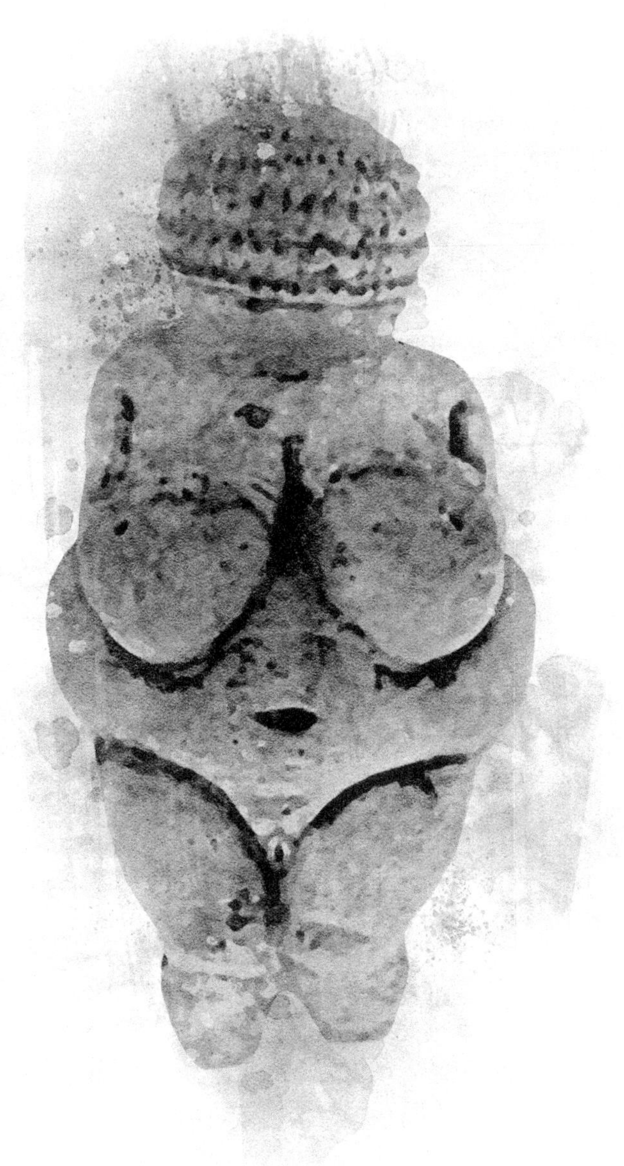

Lesson Two

WHERE HAS SHE BEEN?

"We will never know where, when or by whom the Great Mother was first recognized by humans. Some researchers suggest the Mother Earth concept has existed for more than 200,000 years. Without a doubt she was the first deity. It is an undisputed fact that every human who is alive today is a descendent of a myriad of ancestors who worshiped the Great Mother." — **Rhiannon Cameron, from Goddess Religion, © Rhiannon Cameron, 2000**

PREPARATION FOR TODAY'S LESSON

Breathe deeply ... Exhale and allow yourself to be in this moment. Now take a moment to contemplate your burning questions about The Goddess. Jot them down. See if you find at least some of the answers in today's lesson.

THOUGHTS TO CONSIDER

For most of us, the importance of the Goddess has been downplayed or reduced to brief mentions in social studies classes. It makes you think, she must have been perceived as a pretty great power if such a conscious effort has been made to keep her out of sight and minds!

As we progress in this course, you will find that she has not really been hidden. It is more a case of you not having been taught how to see Her through your spiritual eyes. Today we will explore the question: *How did she disappear from our view*?

Although many historians and archaeologists place the heyday of goddess worship to ancient societies founded thousands of years ago, the feminine divine was actively worshiped as a major deity in ancient cultures just over 2,000 years ago.

UNDERSTANDING THE TIDES OF CHANGE

In order to understand the history of the Goddess and the Divine Feminine (which is sometimes interchangeable with the Sacred Feminine) and figure out how she became hidden or lost, we have to take a look at the history of civilization and religion.

For the most part, all our very ancient ancestors could be considered pagan. The Celts used that word to describe the common folks and farmers who lived in the countryside, and who followed an earth-based spirituality before the Christian stronghold took root. In later years, it was adapted to describe people who practice earth-based traditions and include the worship of a female God or feminine energy as a Divine Force or source.

When ancient man and woman hunted and gathered and survived in tribes, or lived in ancient communities (long before Jesus ever walked the earth) their rituals were likely honoring the mother, the earth, who brought the bounty of substance, and who challenged them at every turn with the conditions of everyday life. As cultures advanced and people dealt with new challenges, they invented ways to see, know, and communicate to the gods/goddesses. This was often through ritual, dancing, drumming, and images.

I encourage you to dive in and do as much additional research as you feel called to. I find it impossible to site the exact, precise moment in time when the Divine Feminine faded from view, and I may be off on some of the dates in the timeline below. My aim is to share my interpretation of historical events to give you a sense of how "Herstory" relates to history. Here is an ever-so-condensed review.

THE VERY ANCIENT GODDESSES

Before the establishment of the religions we know today as the major religions of the world, there were ancient societies known to worship the female divine. One of the most similar and striking finds in archaeological digs of these ancient communities are small clay images of females—the original goddess statues. Famous among them are the Venus of Willendorf, about 25,000 years old, and Goddess of Lespugue which may be 35,000 years old. Both are in museums bearing proof that worship of feminine icons of power existed in cultures around the world.

The Neolithic cultures were rich in these kinds of icons—there were goddesses set about ancient clay ovens and left to watch over children as they slept. Archaeological evidence shows that a complex series or disruptions—including natural disasters and violent invasions—began to shift the world culture and end the reign of the early, peaceful societies governed on the feminine principle.

Some of the world's oldest religions included the Divine Feminine:

- **Hinduism.** Hinduism—a faith that worshiped goddesses 5,000 years ago and continues to—was among one of the earliest religions. There are some people who believe Judaism finds its roots in that faith, as many of the rituals are similar in practice and meaning. The sacred texts of the Hindu Veda's (which honor gods and goddesses) were said to begin around 500 BCE. The Bhagavad-Gita was written about 200 years before Christ was born and it heralded an avatar known as Krishna, who is sometimes thought of today as a Christ-like figure. His consort is Radha, a human woman much like Mary Magdalene who leaves her family to follow Krishna who, by the way, was a cowherd (not so far removed from the concept of "shepherd").

- **Judaism.** It is estimated that Abraham, the father of Judaism, was alive about 2000 years before Christ was born (BCE, Before the Common Era). And that Moses received the Ten Commandments about 700 years later. Prior, there were many Hebrew goddesses in the ancient world. But when Moses brought the Ten Commandments to the Jews and found them dancing around a golden calf (an image, to some, that represented the Egyptian goddess Hathor) he smashed the tablets and had to create them again, along with the Commandment "*Thou shalt have no other Gods before me.*" and "*Thou shalt not make unto thee any graven image.*" There was no mention of a divine consort or the possibility of any other God than the one who is angry and jealous, speaking in a male voice. As a result of the commandments, people of the Jewish faith are taught to worship God through prayer, ritual, chanting, devotion, celebration, et al., but not through images. (However, the mystical aspect of the religion has kept the feminine and includes the Shekhinah, the indwelling, feminine aspect of God. On the Sabbath, she is called the Bride of God).

- **Ancient Mesopotamia.** In the late 500s, the empire of Mesopotamia –which was ruled by goddess Ishtar–was conquered. Formerly the home of Babylon, it is now known as present-day Iraq. Iraq occupies the greater part of the ancient land of Mesopotamia, the plain between Euphrates and Tigris rivers. Some of the world's greatest ancient civilizations were developed in this area. Therefore, the region is often referred to as the "*Cradle of Civilization.*" In the 1990s remains of the ancient temples of the Goddess were still being found. Many of the antiquities were said to be destroyed or compromised in the Iraq war when The National Museum of Iraq in Baghdad was bombed.

- **Early Christianity.** Jews and Pagans were among those being called to and enlightened by Christ in his ministry. Before Jesus made a name for himself, these new recruits were being baptized by John the Baptist. After the death of Jesus, Peter kept the crusade going and became the first Bishop; he was replaced by the more mature and serious Paul, who actually began converting people to the new religion—or so we are told. As the world now knows through interest and investigations stirred by *The Da Vinci Code*, it's conceivable that Mary Magdalene was the wife of Jesus. Many believe she was, at the very least, his spiritual soul mate and first disciple. The down-playing and falsification of her role in the Christ Crusade becomes a glaring example of the sacred feminine being stripped from her place next to Jesus. (Then again, she lived in an era and part of the world where a woman would not be looked upon as an appropriate religious figure, so it would not be too farfetched to consider that the male disciples of Jesus would be "front men" for the new religion).

There are texts that were allegedly removed from the Bible (known as the Gnostic Gospels) and many feminist scholars suspect that ancient scribes spin-doctored the stories of Jesus to delete Mary M., as well as Jesus' devotion to including women as equals in his ministry.

EARLY RELIGIONS ARE TODAY'S "MYTHOLOGY"

Indigenous religions that honored the earth and the Goddess harken back to way before Christ was born and existed in the time of his death. And the religions that have become part of our "mythology" were once important and viable ways of worship in ancient societies.

- **The Romans** had their pantheon of gods and goddesses—Venus, Diana, and Jupiter—and the Greeks had the same cosmic crew known by different names, such as Aphrodite, Athena, and Zeus.

- **The ancient Egyptian religion** dates way back, past 5,000 years, with antiquities of the goddess Isis and son Horus pre-dating the Madonna and child by easily 3,000 years. Just over two thousand years ago, the last Egyptian pharaoh, Cleopatra, worshiped mother goddess Isis and saw herself as a divine female in human form—only thirty-six years before the birth of Jesus Christ. Her beloved Julius Caesar, during his reign, erected temples to the Roman goddess Venus, paying tribute to her as both a love goddess and a mother goddess.

- **The Celts and the Druids in Ireland**, England and Scotland established the wheel of the year which is still used by modern practitioners to chart their year of worship, holy days, and sabbats. In the early days of Celtic Christianity, when the old religion was traded for the new, the Celts did not want to give up their goddesses so they were transformed into martyred saints. For example, goddess Brigid became St. Bridget.

- **Roman Catholicism Sweeps the Land.** Even though the death of Jesus marked the end of the ancient era, there were still holdouts to the old religions. The Roman Catholic Religion was established and solidified by Emperor Constantine, of the same line as Julius Caesar. Through his involvement with the Council of Nicaea (which gathered leaders to convene and make decisions that would change the course of religious history), the church was married to the state and the new religion was set forth as the only religion in the land. New creeds were set forth—such as establishing the holy trinity as the truth, celibacy for priests, and the idea that one can only know God

> through his son, Jesus Christ. When the locals refused to convert, they were converted by the sword and killed. Constantine, himself was a pagan who worshiped the sun god Sol, was not baptized until his dying day. But he followed a dictate that the Roman Catholic faith would unify the people and keep his empire intact.

This practice spread to the Celtic culture where the kings were being advised by the new power that had the ear of the throne—the priests. Over time, the pagans of the countryside were converted to the new faiths as the wheel of the year was adapted as the Catholic Liturgy. Even Christ's birthday, which history tells us was in the summer, was changed to December 25, which was close to the solstice, when the pagan god Sol was celebrated.

While all of this was going on, the Divine Feminine was still part of the pre-Islamic Arabic culture, which had yet to see the birth of the new religion of Islam. There were more than 300 idols in the holy place known as the Kaaba (built by Abraham and Ismail) and, when the new religion was born, they were smashed by the prophet Muhammad and his team. It is said, though, in the centuries before Mohammad was born, Allah was the al-ilah (chief god) and had three daughters, al-Uzza, al-Lat and Manat (considered Goddesses in pre-Islamic Arabia). And of course the Islamic religion is devoted to the one God Allah, and the honoring of the feminine divine is not part of that culture.

WHAT CHANGED THE COURSE OF THE HISTORY?

What caused the end of common worship of the Divine as Feminine? There were so many events it is difficult to pinpoint why or just one. Leonard Schlain, M.D. offered an explanation in *The Goddess vs. the Alphabet* that, to my mind, also makes sense. He contends that as the ancient worlds moved from religion based on images and spiritual ritual, to religion based on the written word, that the right brain cultures shifted to left brain thinking. He says this brought societies into a more male-dominated way of thinking, of living, and eventually to the deletion of the Goddess from the holy writings.

THIS WEEK, TRY THIS

1. Every night, until the next lesson, light a candle of forgiveness for all the ways the Goddess was denied and suppressed in cultures throughout the world. Forgive yourself, also, for any ways you may have ignored her.
2. Say a prayer of celebration and praise, asking her to come to you and reveal your place on the path of the Goddess.
3. Make a list of goddess names you know or can remember and keep it in your journal.

CLOSING THOUGHTS

Don't worry if you cannot wrap your brain around all this. It is a lot to take in! Just make the commitment to create wholeness within yourself and ask the Goddess to help you. See if she speaks to you in daily life by showing you the symbol that came to you in your meditation.

NEXT LESSON

Meet the Goddesses

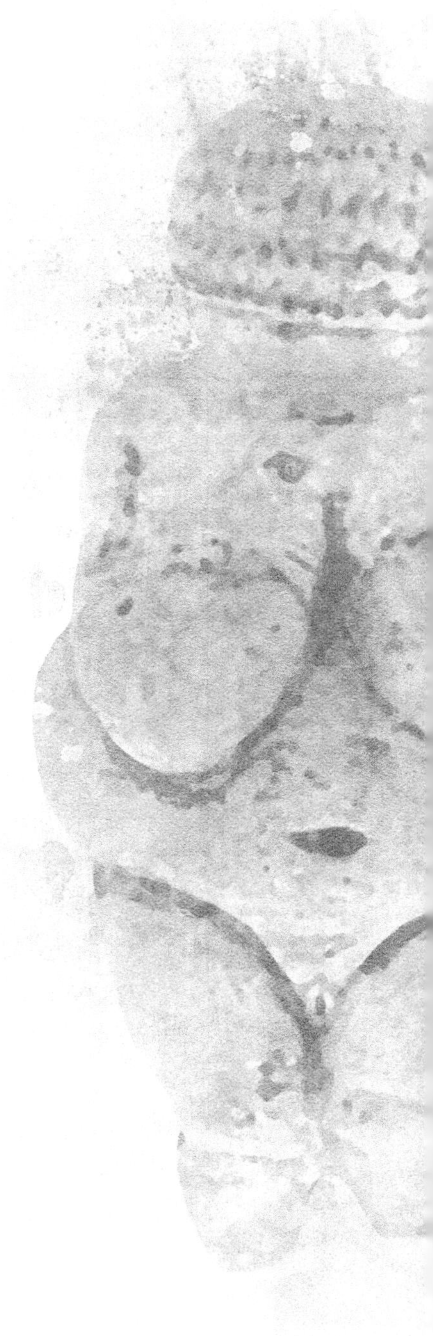

MEET THE GODDESSES

"There are thousands of goddesses, from so many of the world's traditions, known by different names and images, which represent the feminine aspects of divinity and also aspects of our humanity. Their images, energy, and just the mere concept of female divinity can heal us, empower us, instruct us, and help us find our way on life's rocky path."— Laurie Sue Brockway, ***The Goddess Page***

MINDSET PREPARATION

Open now, to a new and renewed awareness of the continued presence of the Goddess in the world's religions and traditions.

THOUGHTS TO CONSIDER

So who exactly is the Goddess and how can you know her by her many facets? Today you will meet a diverse mix of divine females.

FROM THE BEGINNING OF TIME TO NOW

Many people are surprised to learn that goddess history dates back to the earliest civilizations. Our earliest ancestors saw the Divine Feminine as the source of all that is and they depended on her to sustain their very lives. Her power was expressed in the image and, eventually, through stories of thousands of goddesses from cultures around the world.

As time marched on, many of the early goddesses became archetypes for the west. Nike has her own running shoes and clothing line and Athena's name is on everything from a pheromone product to Greek diner menus. Along with Venus—a world-famous goddess, and archetype of love, sexuality, and beauty—they have been relegated to "mythology." But, as Joseph Campbell once reminded us, "One person's mythology is another person's religion." The Goddess was not a myth to our ancestors.

Many of the world's cultures continue to worship, honor and pray to female deities. We will work with some of them in the chapters to come. Other's you can read up on more fully in my book *The Goddess Pages* (Goddess Communications, 2020), which features dozens of Divine Females.

MEET THE GODDESSES:

GODDESS OF ALL THINGS

The Great Goddess. She is the divine female energy of all there is. She represents life itself, death and regeneration and can help transform your relationship with your own mom by connecting with the power of your female ancestry.

AFRICAN AND BRAZILIAN

Oya, Yoruban goddess of wind, hurricane, and wild weather, helps you welcome the winds of change.

Oshun, Macumban Goddess of sensuality, beauty, and womanhood. Helps you tap into your more sensual side and express your sensual self.

Yemaya, West African creation goddess, considered a great and merciful mother. She governs the home and helps women in all things, including childbirth, love, and healing.

BUDDHIST

Kuan Yin, Chinese goddess of healing and compassion, helps you find compassion for yourself and others.

Green Tara, Tibetan Buddhist goddess of protection, helps you feel safe and shows you how to stay calm and centered in a crisis.

White Tara, Tibetan Buddhist goddess of wisdom and healing, helps you heal and find compassion.

CELTIC

Brigid, Celtic goddess of women, poetry, childbirth, and blacksmiths, is a triple goddess who brings inspiration in huge doses.

Maeve, a Celtic/Irish goddess known as a warrior queen, was connected to the legendary, mythical and magical center of Tara. She shows us feminine power and prowess.

CHRISTIAN/GNOSTIC

Mary, mother of Jesus, is not considered a goddess in the Catholic Faith, yet has all the powers of a divine female and is the primary representation of the feminine divine for 2000 years, making her the Spiritual Mother for us all. She helps you connect to your healing power.

Mary Magdalene, the spiritual heroine who is closely linked as sole companion to Jesus, helps you survive the loss of a loved one.

Sophia, goddess of wisdom in Gnostic Christianity, is also referred to in Hebrew texts and the books of Solomon. She helps you tap into, and trust, your own intuition.

HINDU

Lakshmi, Hindu goddess of fortune, gives you a hand, or four, increasing your income, your financial potential, and your ability to plan for your future.

Durga, Hindu mother goddess of protection and war, helps you draw your boundaries and protect yourself from negative energies.

Saraswati, Hindu goddess of wisdom, and creator of the alphabet and literature, she helps you to connect to creative self-expression.

Gauri, Hindu goddess of love and marriage shows you how to get yourself ready for a serious relationship, and how to gently encourage your true love toward the altar.

Kali, Hindu goddess of destruction, known as the black mother. She eats our sins and teaches us to be responsible for our lives.

HEBREW

Lilith, Hebrew goddess, said to be Adam's first wife, was demonized in the Bible but is an empowered woman in Kabbalah and feminine spirituality. She helps you discover your dark and wild side.

Shekhinah, Hebrew goddess, represents the indwelling presence of God. In the Kabbalistic tradition, she is called the, Bride of God or Shabbat Bride, who meets Him on Shabbat, and is considered a divine energy unto herself.

HAWAIIAN

Pele, Hawaiian fire goddess who dwells in the volcano on the Big Island of Hawaii, shows you how to channel and express anger and heal hostility in a healthy way.

Hulu Goddess, sacred feminine guardian of the Hula, awakens the body with spirit and self-expression.

NATIVE AMERICAN

White Buffalo Calf Woman, Native American spirit woman, is the mystical feminine force who taught great sacraments to her people. She helps you connect with the true nature of the soul and create a more peaceful life ... and world.

Butterfly Maiden, Native American spirit woman, takes you from cocoon to butterfly and helps you transform your life.

ANCIENT EGYPTIAN

Isis, Egyptian mother goddess, hailed for her healing, magic and resurrection powers. She helps you rescue troubled relationships and get them back on track.

Hathor, Egyptian goddess of love, beauty, and pleasure, helps you to discover your inner light and shows you how truly beautiful you are.

Bast, Egyptian goddess of play, felines, and females, shows you how to be playful as a pussycat.

Maat, Egyptian goddess of balance and truth, represents the ideals of law, order, and justice. She is seen as a woman with a feather in her headdress and is represented as a feather, because truth is weightless, and light as a feather.

Sehkmet, lion-headed goddess, is one of the most powerful and fierce. She helps us tap into self-protection and express anger.

ANCIENT GREEK

Nike, Greek goddess of victory and herald of success, helps you claim your victories in life.

Artemis, Greek goddess of the hunt, helps you pursue your career goals with passion and focus.

Nemesis, Greek goddess of retribution, helps you handle office politics and troublemakers while helping you see ways you sabotage yourself.

Persephone, Greek goddess of springtime who was abducted by the god of the underworld, shows you how to liberate yourself from bad relationships and set forth a new path in your love life.

The Muses, the nine Greek deities who joyfully presided over the arts, are among the most familiar mythical women and goddesses. They help you celebrate creativity and connections with sisters and friends.

ANCIENT ROMAN

Venus, quintessential Roman goddess of love and beauty, shows you that self-love and appreciation is the first step to embracing your own divinity and empowering your sense of self-worth.

Iris, Roman goddess of the rainbow helps you add color and zest to your life.

Vesta, the Roman Goddess of the hearth, assists you in creating a true home.

NORSE

Freya, Norse goddess of sexual prowess and war, guides you on how to be a man magnet and enjoy every minute of sizzling sexual energy in your life.

Frigg, also a Norse goddess of love and fertility, is married to top god Odin and holds the top job as patron of marriage and motherhood.

SHE IS OMNIPRESENT

The Goddess is multi-faced, multi-faceted, and known by many names. She is as omnipresent and she exists in thousands of forms. In your own spiritual practice, it is time to begin to explore your own personal way of connecting with the Goddess. In the lessons to come, we will call upon specific goddesses representing many different faiths and traditions to help you on all aspects of the spiritual journey to the Goddess.

THIS WEEK, TRY THIS

This week, find some quiet time and return to the place that you began to visit in the first lesson. Let's call it, Our Mother's House. Have a pen and your Goddess Journal ready to jot down any notes after this meditation.

CONNECT WITH HER IN NATURE

Even though Our Mother's House is not a physical place, rather, a place that dwells within you, perhaps one of the best ways to connect with the Goddess is in nature. So try heading into the garden or backyard this week; a short distance to a neighborhood park or nature preserve, or many miles to a favorite natural sanctuary. Wherever you go, pick a place in which you feel serene and secure—a place where you feel "at home."

Begin by finding a comfortable place to sit with few distractions, preferably in the shade. If possible and safe, sit with your back against a tree, allowing your spine to feel the energy of the tree; its strength, endurance, steadfastness through all types of weather, and its natural cycle of seasonal change. Take the time to also ground yourself to the earth, visualizing that the base of your spine is rooted to the earth just like the tree, and be nurtured by the sense of belonging and security.

Begin to take a series of deep cleansing breaths and prepare for meditation. Allow all stress and strain to leave your body and focus on being in the present moment. Close your eyes and allow your breath to return to its normal rhythmic pattern.

Allow yourself to go deeper into relaxation and remember when you are with the Divine Mother you feel safe, protected and warm; you feel well-fed and filled up with spirit. Feel what it is like in Mother's embrace and know that She offers you that kind of love and more.

Set forth a prayer and intention that you will welcome insight and information only from the highest divine source and the divine source most appropriate to you.

When you are feeling centered in that embrace, begin to visualize a figure off in the distance. Slowly watch it approach and see if it takes form. If no image comes to you, allow this energy to manifest as a voice. Listen carefully and see if this being has a message for you.

THEN ASK THIS QUESTION: *HOW CAN I RECOGNIZE YOU IN EVERYDAY LIFE?*

See if you receive a symbol, a word, or a feeling inside. This symbol, sign or sense of knowing will help you connect to the Goddess as you learn more about her in the weeks to come. It may be a symbol you recognize or something completely new. Please note the first thing that comes into your mind during your meditation.

Having experienced this connection to the Goddess, thank Her for the symbol she offered you. Be patient as she walks away, or fades from awareness.

Begin to make your journey back to the present place and time, remembering your observations and expressing gratitude for the opportunity. When you are ready, take three deep cleansing breaths and open your eyes.

Take hold of your pen and jot down the symbol you were given—or draw it—and journal the experience if you feel so moved.

CLOSING THOUGHTS

Stay aware! See if She speaks to you in daily life by showing you the symbol that came to you in your meditation.

NEXT LESSON

Celebrating and Connecting to the Goddess

Lesson Four

CELEBRATING AND CONNECTING TO THE GODDESS

"The Goddess is with each of us every day, embedded deep within our psyches and woven into the very fabric of our lives."
—Sharon Turnbull, Ph.D., author of Goddess Gift

MINDSET PREPARATION

Breathe deeply ... Exhale ... Relax ...

Recall your experience in Our Mother's House—the safe space in which you can connect to the Goddess who dwells within. Set your intention to find the right ways to connect to the energy of the Goddess in daily life, and through special celebrations that draw her nearer to you.

THOUGHTS TO CONSIDER

One of the struggles on the path toward the Goddess is bringing Her down to earth, into our daily lives.

For many of us, She seems removed to the heavens or buried in mythology. For some, it may feel that the spiritual connection to the feminine is harder to find. Those of us who hail from Christian-Judeo religious traditions may grapple with the notion of Goddess because she seems to have been deleted from the spiritual texts and values we were raised with.

A FEMININE "PRESENCE"

If you look closely enough, most religions acknowledge a feminine "presence" that dwells here with us on earth. For example:

- To the Hindus, She is Shakti, the energy that imbues life in both male and female.
- To the Taoists, She is the Tao, the Mother of all things.
- To Tibetan Buddhists, She is Tara, the Mother of All Buddhas.
- To the Christians, She is the Holy Spirit.
- And to the Jews, She is Shekhinah, the indwelling presence of God.

It is important to embrace the Goddess as a universal deity—or as an essence, energy, being, Mother of us all—and approach our work with Her from an all-inclusive perspective.

In this course, you are being introduced to goddesses from an array of different religions and cultures; however, this is simply to give you a diverse selection to explore. The fact that they hail from certain cultures does not mean you must hail from the same place in order to connect with a particular goddess in your life. For example, you do not have to be Greek to love Artemis, or Hindu to love Lakshmi. Feel free to connect to the energy of the Divine Feminine through any goddess that calls to you.

The Goddess lends herself to the spiritual practice of those who are sincere seekers. It is up to you to recognize Her via one or numerous forms, or as Divine Mother of All That Is, and honor Her in the way that feels right for you personally.

To give you a little help, let's explore the kind of occasions that create easier access and deeper experience with the Goddess.

SPECIAL DAYS AND WAYS TO CONNECT

Every tradition offers sacred days devoted to the feminine principle. Ancient religion offered special times to honor the Goddess. The earth-based approach to the Goddess, and the Pagan Wheel of the Year, set forth specific Shabbats and time frames in which our access to the energy of the Goddess becomes more powerful. Culling from numerous sources listed below, here are some of the days and ways in which you can connect to the

Goddess during the course of a week, a month, the whole year.

EVERY MONTH

One of the hallmarks of goddess-based traditions such as Wicca and Celtic Paganism is working with the natural cycles that help you develop an organic connection to the Goddess. Just as the earth is our mother, the moon, too, is considered a representation or aspect of the Divine Feminine. When you follow these moon cycles, you tend to get in sync with the natural rhythms of life. Anyone of any faith can adapt these auspicious times into their calendar.

- **Full Moon**

  Connect to the Goddess at the full moon. In the simplest approach, just stand on Her earth and gaze at her in all her glory in the sky and you will know the energy of the Goddess. This is a favorite time for ritual in many faiths and is an especially auspicious time for all who practice earth-based traditions. On the full moon people gather at all corners of the earth to honor the Goddess, so you are tapping into a full expression of Her energy and the support of those who gather in Her name. It is a time to draw down the power of the moon and a powerful time to bring projects to fruition.

- **New Moon**

  Also known as the "dark moon" it is a time for new beginnings. Begin a new practice, initiate a new goal, make an offering or do a ritual to honor the goddess of new beginnings. In the Jewish faith, this is called Rosh Chodesh, a time for women to gather in community and celebrate the feminine. Hindu's celebrate their New Year festival of Diwali on a new moon and Buddhists celebrate the Chinese New Year on a new moon. The energy of the new moon offers a fresh start every month.

- **Waxing Moon**

  This is the time to build up and develop those things initiated on the new moon. As the moon grows to Her fullness each month you can grow your dreams along with Her cycles.

- **Waning Moon**

  This is a time to release, let go, complete; not a good time to start new things.

- **Menstrual Cycle**

  Shamanic and goddess traditions consider a woman "on her moon" at her most powerful. So powerful is the force of the flow that womenfolk are not allowed to participate in Native American sweat lodges and other spiritual activities. Hindu's do not want menstruating women in the Temple during the first three days. Jews have restrictions on women who are menstruating and require a mikvah bath to cleanse after. While stories have been handed down of women being "unclean" during this time, the truth is that we are just "too powerful." These may be sexist beliefs, but it can also be a time to focus inward and enjoy the natural cycle coursing through you.

NOTE FOR HOT FLASHING FEMALES:

If you are in the peri-menopausal or menopausal years, you might find that as your menstrual cycle tapers off your intuition, clarity and sense of feminine power become heightened. The "flow" and connection to the Goddess comes to you in the form of enhanced wisdom and inner knowing.

- **Every Week**

  Friday is sacred to Venus, the goddess of love, as well as her Norse counterpart Freya and Hindu goddess Lakshmi. This is also the day that people of the Jewish faith welcome the Shekhinah, the "Sabbath Bride." Each Friday brings a fresh opportunity to connect with the Divine Feminine.

- **Wheel of the Year**

  The pagan practitioners observe a calendar known as "The Wheel of the Year." Essentially, it contains 13 full moons and 8 Sabbats, or days of power. There are at least 21 ritual occasions to help bring you closer to the energy and wisdom of the feminine.

THIS MONTH, TRY THIS

1. **Discover the Phases of the Moon**

   Look up the phases of the moon for this year—during this course—and find out a little more about the cycles of each month.

   - For all cycles of the moon, check out the US Naval Observatory website.
   - Find more about full moons and planting cycle through the Farmer's Almanac.
   - Learn about the New Moons.
   - Take a look at the names and meaning of the full moons. They represent powerful times for ritual and honoring the Goddess.

2. **On the Next Full Moon ...**

   Stand beneath the moonlight or sit in a chair by the window where the moon is in view, take a deep breath and read the classic ode to the Divine Mother, *Charge of the Goddess*. The traditional version was written by Doreen Valiente, and adapted here by Starhawk. It is considered a holy prayer for many pagan traditions.

CHARGE OF THE GODDESS

Read the Charge of the Goddess out loud. Written by Doreen Valiente, this is often articulated in goddess spirituality circles to honor and invoke the divine feminine. I am sharing just the first two lines, due to copyright:

Listen to the words of the Great Mother, who of old was called Artemis, Astarte, Dione, Melusine, Aphrodite, Cerridwen, Diana, Arionrhod, Brigid, and by many other names.

Whenever you have need of anything, once a month, and better it be when the moon is full, you shall assemble in some secret place and adore the spirit of Me who is Queen of all the Wise.

You can find the full reading online or in *The Charge of the Goddess - The Poetry of Doreen Valiente*, published by the Centre For Pagan Studies Ltd (February 10, 2014).

CLOSING THOUGHTS

After reading this lesson begin your moon research. Jot down all the full moons and new moons for the next year in your appointment book. This way you will know when they will occur. Begin to notice the rhythms of the feminine and your personal connection to her as you draw her closer to you in daily life. Begin to plan life around Her schedule and become more in sync with nature.

NEXT LESSON

Meet Aurora, Roman Goddess of the Dawn
and New Beginnings

Lesson Five

MEET AURORA, ROMAN GODDESS OF THE DAWN AND NEW BEGINNINGS

"The goddess Dawn, rosey-fingered, arose to bring the light to the gods and the mortals."— **Homer, The Iliad**

MINDSET PREPARATION

Breathe deeply and let out a yawn as you stretch out your arms and stretch your back. Then closes your eyes for a moment and envision the sun in all its glory rising out of the horizon.

The ancient Romans believed in the power of Aurora to bring the morning light. Even today, everything looks clearer after a good night's sleep.

THOUGHTS TO CONSIDER

No matter what kind of work you are doing at this time, you have a personal path that is uniquely your own. Each and every one of us has a calling, something we believe in, a mission that gives our lives a sense of a purpose and meaning. When you stand at the threshold of transition (e.g., feeling restless where you are, searching for a new job, getting laid off, or fired, wanting to start a new business), that is when a true path can most clearly be revealed to you. It is then that you can see the light just before the dawn.

FINDING YOUR TRUE PATH IN LIFE

A true path is as personal and individual as a fingerprint. It's not about competing with others, or following cultural trends; it's about being your best and calling forth your own unique talents, abilities, and style.

Whether you find your *true path* as a hair stylist (who interacts with thousands of people and makes each and every one of them feel better about themselves when they leave your chair), or as an author (who writes books that change people's lives), having a sense of mission in life is what inspires us to joyously get up in the morning and go to work. *And* to work with dedication even when the going gets rough.

Honor your path in life, and you will always find your way back to work that gives deeper meaning to your life.

It may seem unsettling not knowing where you're heading ... but this is where the magic of new beginnings dwells. Like the night gently turning to day, each experience will very naturally lead to the next leg of the journey, while urging you to birth the woman you are meant to be.

AURORA, ROMAN GODDESS OF NEW BEGINNINGS

Aurora is a goddess who can help you find your way in the world because she brings dawn through the darkness and represents proof that tomorrow is another day. She reveals your next steps as she "raises night's veil" and opens the door to possibilities not seen or known the day before. She represents the dawning of new beginnings, fresh opportunities and new ways of seeing things.

Aurora, the Roman goddess of the dawn, is also known as "Light." She was "Eos" to the Greeks. To the ancients, she was "the rosey-fingered dawn with the snowy eyelids bringing the first glimmer of the day." It was her job to lead her brother,

Helios, the sun god, into the new day, thus every morning she rose from the ocean into the sky. Sometimes she traveled as a winged goddess tilling an urn from which fell the morning dew; sometimes she was mounted on Pegasus, the winged horse. But it was believed, most commonly, that she rode in a purple chariot drawn by two horses.

Her husband was Tithonus, a mortal who was made immortal, but not given the anti-aging powers of the gods and thus became a shriveled elderly man. Perhaps because of her "situation" at home, she was notorious for chasing and seducing young men. Symbolically, her husband was the "old" she left behind in bed each night and the young men were the "youthful energy" that she chased like the new day. She is often pictured as a wispy, airy, beautiful woman in white, or barely any clothing; and she is sometimes seen on chariot streaking across the sky.

LET HER ILLUMINATE YOUR PATH

Aurora is also the well-known term for the spectacular display of Northern and Southern Lights (aurora borealis and aurora australis), which Webster's calls, "a luminous phenomenon that consists of streamers or arches of light appearing in the upper atmosphere of a planet's magnetic polar regions." They streak across the sky from horizon to horizon as if they are Aurora herself making that early morning sky trek.

You may not be in a part of the world where you can see the lights named after the goddess of dawn but just imagine that she lives in all stars. Before you sleep, look out upon the starry night in whatever way you can—from a back porch or a window—and make a wish for illumination about the life path you are to pursue.

As you lay your head down for the night, Aurora rests in the dark skies and twinkling stars getting ready to flee once again to begin a brand new day—filled with new possibilities for passion and aliveness. Aurora goes to bed with the sleepy night, but when she awakens, the world is transformed. To meet the dawn and greet new professional possibilities, try this exercise when you are contemplating a job, or career change, or are in transition in your business life. This will help you tune into Aurora's energies in the most effective way and inspire you to declare a personal mission statement for your life and life's work. It is good to define your personal mission at every stage: expect that over time you will rewrite it and make adjustments.

THIS WEEK, TRY THIS

1. Take a warm bath to cleanse the body, mind, and soul. Clear away the energies of the day with a warm, relaxing bath. Turn off the television, tune out the world, give yourself a silent bedtime so that your mind is clear and new insights can arise. Review the stresses of the day and one by one release them into the warm water. When the bath is done and you pull the plug, intend that all of the day's disappointments go down the drain with the water.
2. Go to bed with a prayer to the Goddess. For example:

   Dearest Aurora, goddess of dawn,
   Please bring illumination in early morn.
   As you awaken at your twilight hour,
   Let me feel your energy and power.

3. Awaken gently, before the dawn. It has been said that the greatest power of the day lives in the moments between night and day, around 4:30 a.m. This is when Aurora readies for her streak from night to day, a time when nothing else stirs. It is the time when many writers awaken to write, successful business people awaken to start their day, and when monks rise to pray. Challenge yourself to awaken at this hour, when nothing else is stirring, and allow Aurora to come to you. Awakening at this time as a

practice helps instill discipline and gives you a chance to start the day when a new day is truly breaking.

4. Be still and listen to her whispers as she transforms night to day. If you are a coffee or tea drinker, go ahead make your morning brew. You might as well utilize your normal caffeine buzz in an inspiring way. (Fruit juice is just as fine). Sit quietly and sip. If you sit for twenty minutes, as the new day dawns, sipping your coffee or tea, a million ideas will flow to you. Jot down any inspiration or ideas that come to you.
5. Write a mission statement for your life's work/career. Every organization has a mission statement that is their guiding light and you can too. Before the next day's dawn, ask yourself the questions, "what do I believe in?" and "how do I want to express myself in the world?" Formulate a mission statement for your life's work/career. Include qualities you want to experience, things you hope to achieve and do, promises about how you will conduct yourself. Make it as specific as you are willing, but leave room for evolution and give yourself permission to be living a life that is still a work in progress. Crafting a personal mission statement can help establish a rhyme and reason to your life and help steer you along your true path. For example:

   "I will do work I love to do in the field of publishing. I will bring compassion and open-heartedness to my work, even in the face of difficulties. I will earn more than enough money, yet money will never be my only motivation for working. I will be passionate, committed and dedicated. I will be grateful for all my success, and will not take rejection personally. I will build a body of work I can be proud of and write things that touch people's lives. People will know my name and recognize me for my contributions."

6. Honor the twilight time of transition, the time between then and now.

It's important to appreciate the time in between an ending and new beginning; it's a point of power for any journey.

CLOSING THOUGHTS

Spend the time between now and the next lesson appreciating and observing the natural transformations of time—day to night, night to morning, morning to afternoon—and begin to come into sync with the natural rhythms of the day.

NEXT LESSON

Meet Shekhinah, Hebrew goddess
who dwells with us on Earth

Lesson Six

MEET SHEKHINAH, HEBREW GODDESS WHO DWELLS WITH US ON EARTH

"The Bible began with a powerful acknowledgement of the dual nature of the Source of Being. But by chapter two of Genesis, Elohim was thought of as singular and male. When Eve did not obey "Him," she was cursed with male domination. And the Divine Feminine shared Eve's fate. Eve's story marked the end of the reign of the Queen of Heaven ..." — **Miki Raver, author, Listen to Her Voice**

MINDSET PREPARATION

Breathe deeply... Exhale... And relax. Allow yourself to just be. Then begin today's lesson with this invocation:

"O Queen of Heaven and Earth Holy Shekhinah, we open our minds and hearts and lives to you, And pray you enter and indwell."
— From "Invocation to the Holy Shekhinah," the Gnostic Gospels

THOUGHTS TO CONSIDER

Do you realize how empowered you would be if you truly felt that God/Goddess walked the earth with you ... is with you at every moment ... is there for you through every challenge and every victory?

Those of us who have been let down by past religious training and spiritual influences, or have gotten smacked around by life enough to question the existence of the Divine, sometimes find it hard to believe we can partner with the Divine. More surprising is the notion that, according to the Jewish tradition, God walks among us in feminine form. She is known as Shekhinah. Shekhinah is a Hebrew goddess who dwells with us on earth.

REDISCOVERING SHEKHINAH

Although many people do not realize or recognize this, the Divine Feminine was associated with Judaism from the most ancient times. And, according to Jewish historian Raphael Patai, she played an important part in the religion, taking many forms for a long time. Since Judaism is a monotheistic religion strongly connected to a patriarchal God, we sometimes forget or look past the feminine aspect of God. Shekhinah is a Talmudic term describing the manifestation of God's presence on earth.

You don't have to be Jewish to appreciate Shekhinah. She is a Divine Feminine or Divinely Feminine energy, that is universal and accessible to all.

WHO IS SHEKHINAH?

Shekhinah, (pronounced sheh-kee-NAH), is the consort—or bride of God. And in that respect, is considered Mother to us all—just as God is our Father. From the traditional Jewish point of view, Shekhinah is the majestic presence or manifestation of God which has descended to "dwell" among men and women. She is the energy of God that lives, breathes and walks among the people.

Historically, Shekhinah has also been a term used to refer to the energy of God that dwelt in the Tabernacle (or holiest of temples) with the Jewish people. It is said that when Moses asked to see God, it was Shekhinah that he saw—the belief being that one could not see God in His fullness, but could see Shekhinah as an "emanation of God." From the perspective of Kabbalah and mystical Judaism, she plays a dual role as one of the emanations of God *and* the actual Presence of God. The name Shekhinah is derived from the Hebrew verb *sakan* or *shachan*. In Biblical Hebrew, the word means literally to *settle, inhabit,* or *dwell,* and is used frequently in the Hebrew Bible.

Interestingly, the Shekhinah in the New Testament is commonly equated to the presence or indwelling of the Spirit of the Lord. In Christianity, she would be "Holy Spirit." In earth-based worship cultures, she has been adapted in her own right as a Divine Female or Jewish goddess.

HER KABBALISTIC MYTHOLOGY

Rabbi Joseph Gelberman was the founder of The New Synagogue in New York and author of the book: *Kabbalah, As I See It*. He shared the Kabbalistic point of view that when Adam and Eve left the garden, the Feminine Divine went with them, to comfort them and keep them company:

> *The creator was divided by an inner conflict about how to deal with Adam and Eve. God's children had disobeyed his only commandment: Do not eat of the tree of knowledge or taste of good and evil. One part of the divine insisted on punishing Adam and Eve. The other part of the divine, the Shekhinah, that expresses the feminine qualities of God, suggested they should not be punished because they were merely innocent, curious children and this was their first transgression. The quarrel continued for a while. The part of God that insisted punishment—exile from the Garden of Eden—did not waver. When the Shekhinah insisted just as firmly that the punishment was too great for innocent children, the part that sought punishment said to the Shekhinah, "In that case, you go with them."*

"This" he says, "is how the Shekhinah came to be God's presence among the people of earth."

THIS WEEK, TRY THIS

1. **Honor Her on Friday**
   The tradition of the Sabbath bride continues to this day. On Fridays, it is the women who light the Shabbat candles with a prayer. Then everyone welcomes Shekhinah to the Shabbat (Sabbath) dinner.

2. **Have a Spiritual Gathering**
   The Zohar, the book of Mystical Judaism says, "One must prepare a comfortable seat with several cushions and embroidered covers, from all that is found in the house, like one who prepares a canopy for a bride. For the Shabbat is a queen and a bride." It is believed one must sing and rejoice at the table in her honor. One must receive the lady with many lighted candles, many enjoyments, beautiful clothes, and a house embellished with many fine appointments.
   - Prepare a small feast, or a potluck dinner, with women friends, or all friends, if you like!
   - Have a Sabbath candle tree (that holds multiple candles) or several candle holders and give each woman present a chance to light one candle and say a prayer for themselves and families, silently or out loud.
   - Celebrate by sharing a meal, at a table that has a place reserved for Her.
   - Take in the joy and peace of sharing your Friday night with friends and Shekhinah.

3. **Offer a Prayer to Draw Her Nearer**
   This beautiful prayer comes from the prayer book of The New Synagogue: The Synagogue for Spiritual Judaism, founded and led by the late Rabbi Joseph Gelberman, and co-led by Rabbi Roger Ross.

The Sun on the treetops is no longer seen.
Come gather to welcome the Sabbath, our Queen.
Behold her descending. The holy. The blessed.
And with Her the angels of peace and rest.
Draw near, and here abide.
Draw near, draw near, O Sabbath Bride.
Peace also to you, you angels of peace.

4. **A Hymn for Her**

   At the highest and most mystical level, each Friday can bring a spiritual marriage or renewal of marriage. As God is reunited with His feminine aspect, we reunite with Her as well. Women can symbolically marry the goddess within; men can connect to their feminine sides. This excerpt from a traditional hymn inspires us to honor the feminine and tells us in doing so we more fully connect to love, joy and the Divine pleasures.

"I sing in hymns to enter the gates of the Field of holy apples.

A new table we prepare for Her, a lovely candelabrum sheds its light upon us.

Between right and left the bride approaches, in holy jewels and festive garments.

Her husband embraces Her in Her foundation, giving Her pleasure, squeezing out his strength.

Torment and trouble are ended. Now there are joyous faces and spirits and souls.

He gives Her great joy in twofold measure.

Light shines upon Her and streams of blessing."

—From Hymn for the Sabbath Eve (Friday Sundown), by Rabbi Isaac Luria, the Ari Zaal (Safed Spirituality, Lawrence Fine, Translator, Paulist Press, 1984)

5. **Connect with Her on the New Moon**

   Rosh Chodesh is an almost forgotten cultural tradition that has seen a great revival in recent times. Jewish women around the world embrace the feminine on the night of the new moon, each month. It is customary for women to gather together to honor renewal. Many modern women use this time for fresh starts and new beginnings, to reconnect to their faith and to the feminine. Like the Sabbath, it is a time out from a hectic world and demanding schedule. While Jewish women connect with the energy of the ancestors and celebrate this as a sacred time to connect to other Jewish women, this day can be claimed as sacred for women of all faith backgrounds.

CREATE A COMMUNITY

Consider celebrating with friends, in a manner similar to the suggested Friday night feast. It is also a great time to focus together on peace—for your lives and the world.

OFFER THIS PRAYER:

Sacred Mother, Shekhinah, bring your brilliant light through the dark of this new moon.
Please bring to us your sacred presence and help restore us in this sacred time.
Let us be strong, together, as we prepare for the times ahead.
Bring peace to our lives, our loved ones, our souls.
And bring peace, please, to our world.
Shine your light on the troubles.
In the spirit of Tikkun Olum, help us do our part to heal and perfect the world.
Guide over us and give us strength
Walk with us, as we do our part for peace.
© Rev. Laurie Sue Brockway

CLOSING THOUGHTS

It is time to create wholeness within ourselves but, to put it simply; it is time to listen to our Divine Mother. See if she speaks to you, shows you images or shares wisdom with you in daily life.

NEXT LESSON

Meet Amaterasu & Uzume, Shinto Goddesses
of Beauty, Laughter & Joy

Lesson Seven

MEET AMATERASU & UZUME, SHINTO GODDESSES OF BEAUTY, LAUGHTER & JOY

"The Playful Goddess Ama No Uzume would dance by the entrance of the cave, making notions and faces that would bring such a laughter from those who watched Her that curiosity of Amaterasu would be aroused enough to open the door and peer out."
—Merlin Stone, from Ancient Mirrors of Womanhood, Volume II

PREPARATION FOR TODAY'S LESSON

Take a deep breath and gently exhale saying, "ha ha ha."

Repeat: ha ha ha ha ha ha ha ha.

Again: tee hee hee hee ha ha ha ha ha ha snort.

Are you smiling now? Begin this lesson with a board smile and an open heart.

THOUGHTS TO CONSIDER

We have all had those days when everything that can go wrong does go wrong. When the check is not in the mail, the dog pees on the rug, and the dry cleaner lost your favorite shirt. It is very easy to get frustrated, bent out of shape, and lose your sense of humor. There are a lot of things in life that can lead us down a bumpy, grumpy path. But there is one thing that can snap us out of it in a nanosecond: Laughter. You can do it with anyone safely, and it's mess free, drug-free, and it doesn't require a condom. A good laugh, like a good orgasm, alleviates tension and makes you feel good all over.

KEEPING LIFE LIGHT AND FILLED WITH LAUGHTER

Laughter is like medicine and studies show that when we laugh, physiologically, it is impossible to be depressed or sad. Like a quick fix of fun and an easy to access a mood elevator, it helps uplift us and heals us. Even if you are not in the mood to laugh, the act of laughing will make you laugh. Then you can see there is an entire world around you just waiting to give you a good hoot and to point out the hilarity of being divinely human.

We all need comical relief, and time out from tragedy and challenge. We can help heal ourselves—and our friends and family—with humor and laughter. If you, or anyone you know, are suffering from humor deprivation, it's time to have a good laugh. It costs nothing, yet helps you gain a new attitude and perspective. Laughter brings sunshine into your life. No matter how bad things get, or how awful they may seem, your world can change with the simple move of your facial muscles—a slight twitch of your lips that starts as a smile and grows into a big, loud, hilarious laugh.

UZUME AND AMATERASU

Uzume and Amaterasu are Japanese goddesses who can help you, your friends and even random strangers have a good laugh. They help you see the importance of laughter as well as the hilarity in life; they show you the ease of laughing out loud with friends and the way it can change the world. Together, they assist in returning us to sunshine and smiles. They represent lightening up and having a good guffaw.

IMPORTANT JAPANESE GODDESSES

Omikami Amaterasu and Ama No Uzume are important Japanese goddesses who are worshiped actively today by practitioners of the Shinto faith, in Japan and elsewhere. Their destinies were entwined and friendship sealed when Uzume helped Amaterasu through a dark moment in time and healed her—and the world—with laughter.

- Amaterasu is the supreme deity of the Shinto religion. The Japanese people honor Amaterasu and have temples erected to her throughout the country. Her name means "Great Shining Heaven" and it's said that rice cannot grow without her because she is the Queen of all Kami (the natural forces of the earth). She is considered mother to all the emperors of Japan; all royal families trace their roots to her. Shinto temples honor her with beautiful, big mirrors because it is believed her spirit enters the mirror so she can be there for all ceremonies and blessings. Her holiest shrine in all Japan is the huge sacred mirror at the Ise Shrine of Amaterasu Omikami, a humble wooden temple on the Banks of the Ise Wan.
- Uzume is a shameless and joyful exhibitionist, wild and wacky in her attempt to get a good laugh. Uzume was a voluptuous and bawdy goddess of merriment and she was also a shaman. Shamans and diviners were important to the Japanese as healers and oracles. In modern renditions, the goddesses are depicted as Japanese women. Amaterasu is calm, regal and soft looking, while Uzume is seen in a wild dance, usually not fully clothed. Amaterasu is also depicted as a sacred mirror.

THE LAUGHING MYTH

The story of the day the sun went away is supposed to be a humorous tale. Amaterasu's brother Susano-O, the wind god, got drunk, acted like a jerk and defiled her temples and rice fields. She pleaded with him to stop making a mess, and he refused. Amaterasu withdrew to a cave and the world was plunged into darkness; it grew cold. All her sibling gods and goddesses pleaded with her to bring sunshine back; she wouldn't budge and they were stressed because the world was a mess without the sunshine. They asked the wild and risqué Uzume to intervene.

As a shaman, Uzume was unafraid to dance into the darkness; as a goddess of merriment, she was wild and would do anything for a laugh. She stripped naked, and covered herself with flowers and plants; she then turned over a washtub, hopped up and did a lewd dance, and simultaneously drummed the healing sound of the shaman with her feet atop the tub. In the fervor of divine ecstasy, she lifted off the plants, flowers and exposed herself. All the deities in the vicinity laughed hysterically; they were hooting and hollering. Amaterasu, hearing the wild cheers and laughter, couldn't resist. She peeked out from her cave. A mirror had been placed behind Uzume, and when Amaterasu saw her own beauty for the first time, with a big smile on her face, she was dazzled. Laughing hysterically with the rest of the cosmic crew, she vowed never to go away again.

THIS WEEK, TRY THIS

Try some simple ways to bring their laughter and sunshine to everyday life:

1. Greet the Rising Sun. One of Amaterasu's emblems, the rising sun, appears on Japan's national flag. People in Japan welcome her with prayers and hand clapping each morning. This can be a stimulating warm up to the start of

a new day. Just the act of clapping will be a wake-up call to your body. Clapping makes you feel happy and joyous!

2. Share laughter and light with friends. You don't have to be outrageous as Uzume. Friends can share a laugh together over the most mundane and silly things. From rural areas to urban cities, in the middle of Manhattan to a farm on Montana, we can always gather with a friend or two to express gratitude for a new day's sun and share some laughter.
3. Share a meal. Just one breakfast meeting a week with people of a similar sense of humor is great medicine for the soul. Order your meal, say thanks for a new day, and celebrate by sharing laughs, cracking jokes, and being goofy. You can have joke contests and funny storytelling fests. If you are not good joke tellers, buy a book of jokes and practice on each other. Stay in touch with your friends during the week by e-mailing each other the best Internet humor you can access.
4. Create a deck of "Happy Cards." Buy a pack of plain index cards and some pretty magic markers and write individual sayings, jokes, and quotes that make you laugh and bring sunshine to your life and to others. Keep them in a special box, or a decorated coffee can, and reach in any time you need a laugh. Offer them to friends, like brownies, when they come to visit. Even if they laugh at you for having "Happy Cards" in a coffee can it is worth the effort.
5. Start a good mood virus. If you long to be the ultimate fun bunny and favorite friend that everyone wants to be around, take responsibility for spreading good cheer. Uzume didn't just get Amaterasu laughing—she had all the deities in stitches. When we allow ourselves to feel good and filled with joy, we radiate it. Just as our bad

moods can be contagious, our good moods can pave the way for many miles of smiles. If we smile, people smile back; if we laugh, they chuckle too!

6. Laugh like crazy with Uzume. When Uzume did her wacky dance, she wasn't thinking "what will the other goddesses and gods think of me?" She was focused on bringing the sunshine back. Outrageous and out there, she got everyone laughing—and you can too without lifting your skirt (unless you want to of course)! If you are with a small group of friends who are not feeling too peppy, or just one bummed out buddy, and you want to break the bad mood ... start laughing.

   This is not something you would do at a funeral, but in a non-emotionally charged situation where the room, and people in it, need a new burst of energy and sunshine. Break out in laughter. Start slowly with a straight face, so they don't even know what you are up to. Then formulate a smile ... then turn it into a chuckle ... then build into a contagiously happy laugh. They will think you are insane at first until they can resist no more ... the laughter will sneak up on them and out of them. Just keep laughing like crazy and see if one person can resist the allure of that wild laughter. It will fill the room with a burst of laughter and sunshine!

7. Write down 9 fun things you can do between now and the next lesson (can be anything from renting a funny movie to going out to fly a kite!)

CLOSING THOUGHTS

Ready, get set, throw your head back and let it roar! Laugh for twenty seconds!

Ha ha ha ha ha ha ha ha hee hee hee hee hee hee ha ha ha ha ha ha ha ha ...

Now, didn't that feel great? A good laugh a day keeps the darkness away.

NEXT LESSON

Meet White Tara, Tibetan Buddhist
Goddess of Compassion

Lesson Eight

MEET WHITE TARA, TIBETAN BUDDHIST GODDESS OF COMPASSION

Sprung from Divine Tears
First Named Wisdom Moon
Vowed To Attain Enlightenment
Only In Female Form
To Rescue Us from All Fear
Remove All Obstacles
And Transform the World of Suffering
Into the World Of Peace.
See her coming to you, gleaming,
Seated on the full moon.
— **Auntie Matter, posted at WhiteTara.com**

PREPARATION FOR TODAY'S LESSON

Breathe deeply and exhale ... Breathe out any fear or tension you may be feeling just now. Breathe in white healing light. Exhale ... Relax. Allow yourself to just be in the moment.

You might listen to a White Tara Mantra on You Tube to set the mood for this lesson.

The meaning of this chant will become clear as you proceed with today's lesson.

THOUGHTS TO CONSIDER

We live in times so challenging that stress, fear, tears, and disease have become "normal." Distress is a regular part of our waking hours, and it seeps into our dreams as well. There seems to be no real "time out" from sadness in our world. It takes a lot to remain strong and centered.

Somehow, even the small bumps in the road of life can seem huge when you are under pressure or not feeling your best. The big issues and world-wide problems seem insurmountable. It is very hard to live an enlightened life if you feel weighed down by the world, pressures in your own life, or illness and imbalance in mind or body.

EMBRACE HEALING AND WHOLENESS

Tara is a goddess who pours compassion and healing onto all the wounds of the world and helps you heal your deepest pain and fear. She is the one to call to when you are having a spiritual crisis, coping with illness or feel lost in despair. She is a merciful mother who will put her arms around you when you feel sick, tired, worn out. She will not judge you; she will only seek to bring peace and balance, which will, in turn, bring healing and wholeness.

TARA, GODDESS OF COMPASSION

White Tara is the Tibetan Buddhist goddess of compassion. She is sometimes called the Mother of all Buddhas because she represents the motherly aspect of compassion and also represents the essence of the three Buddhas. Her white color signifies purity, wisdom, and truth. It is believed that her love heals the source of all disease in our bodies, lives, and our world, and that she brings us health, strength, longevity, and inner beauty. She is worshiped in a rainbow of colors based on various aspects of her legend and attributes, but the White and Green Tara of the Tibetan Tantric tradition are the most recognizable forms.

The root of Tara's name is the sound "tri" meaning "to cross." When we call upon Tara she immediately comes to us, pouring compassion and love on any situation. White Tara is often seen on Tibetan holy art as a mature, white-skinned female.

Her posture is one of grace and calm. Her right hand makes the boon-granting gesture and her left hand is in the protective mudra. In her left hand, White Tara holds an elaborate lotus flower that contains three blooms. This is symbolic of her relationship to the three Buddhas. She represents compassion in action and is said to also help us cross from suffering to happiness and to grant wishes.

THE MYTHOLOGY OF TARA

There are two legends about her origins. The mythic legend is that she was born from the tears shed by Avalokiteshvara, the Buddha of compassion, as a gift to end the suffering of all creation. The tears trickling down the left side of the Buddha's face formed the motherly and mature "White Tara" and the salty drops on the right birthed the fearless and youthful "Green Tara."

The other legend is very similar to Chinese Buddhist Goddess Kuan Yin. It tells us that she was a human princess who lived a life of total service, compassion, and the highest spiritual aspiration. She dedicated herself to serving the Buddhist monks. The monks told her that because of her path, she earned the right to be reborn in male form and teach the ways of the Buddha. She told them that since the concepts of male and female were only an illusion, she would remain in female form until all of humanity was liberated from illusion and reached enlightenment.

THIS WEEK, TRY THIS

1. Chanting. It is believed that Tara's protection and favors may be instantly received just by calling her name or chanting her mantra:

"OM TARE TUTTARE TURE SOHA"
Pronounced" "Ohm Tar-re Tu-Ta-re Tu-ra So-ha"

It means "Hail Tara ... Her enlightenment and compassion protects me and liberates me from external fears and internal delusion ... may I honor this in myself!"
Chant this to yourself nine times before you go to bed and nine times when you awake. Whenever you feel ill, off balance, upset you can call to the Goddess with this chant. Always do it nine times.

2. Buy or download her image. Keep it by your bed and gaze at her while you chant her Mantra.
3. Send your worries to her on the smoke of incense. Daily devotion to her can include the burning of Tara or Nag Champa incense next to her likeness. Buddhists believe prayers are taken to the heavens on smoke. Speak what is in your heart and tell her what you need to heal. You can make it an offering: "Mother Tara, I give to you my burdens, my fears, my imbalances, and my aches and pains ... please take them, mother, and transform them and heal them so that I can feel good again." You can burn away all cares and worries, surrendering them to the Goddess, for she can take them, and more.
4. Get a mani stone. It carries the sacred mantra, "Om Mani Padme Hum," inscribed on smooth stone plates, pebbles, and rocks. Tibetans leave them as offerings or place them as blessing stones in front of the home or inside. There are small pocket size versions too. It is meant to connect you to the sacred energy. You can also skip the stone and just offer the chant. It is pronounced: *Ohm Mah Nee Pahd May Hum.*

   Some experts say it cannot be translated into English but many people interpret the chant as "I call to you, Jewel of the Lotus."

CLOSING THOUGHTS

White Tara is a Bodhisattva who has vowed to return to this world until all sentient beings have reached enlightenment. Tibetan Buddhists call to her and praise her for healing, wholeness, and enlightenment. Feel free to call to her too!

NEXT LESSON

Meet Lakshmi, Hindu Goddess of Good Fortune

Lesson Nine

MEET LAKSHMI, HINDU GODDESS OF GOOD FORTUNE

"Lakshmi is the divine form of the empowered woman. While she is a wife and mother, she is an independent deity worshipped in her own right."

—D. Debroy, from Lakshmi Puja

MINDSET PREPARATION

Breathe deeply ... Exhale. Relax and find your center. Now open your arms wide—to each side—and affirm, "I am OPEN to receive all the good and abundance of the Universe."

With an open mind and heart begin today's lesson.

THOUGHTS TO CONSIDER

Having money flowing to and through our lives is a priority for most of us. We need it to pay bills and survive. If we want to fulfill our dreams and create a life of our own choosing, we have to have the wherewithal to get there financially. It is important to do things in life that increase earning potential, as well as help you save money, balance finances, and build a healthy financial future.

FINDING MATERIAL AND SPIRITUAL WEALTH

Prosperity, however, is not just about money. Financial satisfaction and stability are a part of prosperity, yet true prosperity is having wealth that is material and spiritual and living a life that is rich in all things—including love, security, friendship, opportunity, work you love, spiritual growth, and development. Having enough money, or more than enough, for many people, goes hand in hand with having balance in their lives and an appreciation of all of life's gifts.

Lakshmi is a goddess you can turn to if you need help with finances, a job, success, happiness, and love. *Lakshmi, by name, means fortune*. She offers the special powers and richness that most humans will agree they need, desire, and pray for—good fortune, both material and spiritual.

LAKSHMI, KNOWN FOR BRINGING GOOD THINGS TO LIFE

Lakshmi is the Hindu Goddess of Good Fortune and Beauty. She represents and is seen as the personification of abundance, prosperity, wealth, well-being, and harmony. She is actively worshiped daily by millions of Hindus, and interfaith practitioners of goddess spirituality, around the globe. Even the poorest of the poor believe in her.

Because of her popularity, she is considered a universal goddess. Lakshmi, like many Hindu deities, is often pictured as a beautiful Indian woman with big dark eyes and with four arms. Clad in a sari, in a form that is very feminine and full, she sits or stands on her lotus throne. She usually has two lotuses, in either of her back hands. Her front arms offer blessings and what are known as "boons" or favors.

Her ability to enhance your good fortune in life is symbolized by the gold coins that you see pouring from her hands back into the ocean of life. Lakshmi's mate is the Lord Vishnu—known as the Great Preserver, who comes to earth in the form of important avatars, such as Krishna.

Lakshmi is cohorts with Ganesha, Lord of Obstacles; they often work side by side. This is indicated by the frequency with which you see their icons and pictures together. Ganesha clears the path of anything in the way of fortune. He removes obstacles so Lakshmi can deliver fortune into your life.

THE MYTHOLOGY OF LAKSHMI

Lakshmi has one of the most colorful creation myths of all the deities in the Hindu pantheon. It is said goddess Lakshmi was born, fully grown, on a pink lotus that rose from the milky sea. She was immediately bedecked, bejeweled and worshiped by the gods and sages. They prayed that she would come to their abodes, and to their worlds, for they believed that where Lakshmi is you will also find riches and fulfillment.

Three millennia later, long after her story was first told, people still believe that where there is wealth, there is Lakshmi—and that inviting Lakshmi into their lives will attract wealth on all levels. She comes alive in homes and temples everywhere. "Believers" of all faiths trust that praying to the *Goddess of Fortune* brings all things good to life. As the symbol of all things fortunate, she is a highly sought after and beloved female deity.

It is believed that those who pay attention to the *Goddess of Fortune* every day develop a clear channel of communication with Her. The Hindu culture is thousands of years old and layered with various ways to worship Lakshmi. You can also approach her by connecting with the "energy" of the Goddess in a way that fits with your personal spiritual practice. Lakshmi reaches beyond religion and Divine "typecasting" and into the hearts of and souls of everyday people.

Lakshmi exists in a dimension far beyond our human struggles and sadness. From where she sits on her Sacred Lotus, she can guide us to greater fortune, deeper love relationships and more joy. Because she is also considered a Great Mother Devi (goddess) she can guide us from darkness, into the light. In fact, if you allow Lakshmi to be present in your life, you just might find she elevates you to a higher state of being and living. And in that state, you will begin to see that you can create anything!

THIS WEEK, TRY THIS

1. Attend a Lakshmi Puja: In the culture from which Lakshmi hails, she is treated with great reverence and devotion. In the United States, it is very easy for anyone to attend, or even sponsor (request) a Lakshmi Puja, which is a form of formal worship to the Goddess.

   Anyone of any faith can have a Hindu priest perform a puja at a temple or private home. You can also attend what is usually called a Sri MahaLaxmi or Sri MahaLakshmi (meaning Mother Lakshmi) Abishekam, which is the sacred purification and washing of the goddess with milk, yogurt, honey, and more. The 108 names of the goddess are chanted, and prayers are uttered repeatedly during a Lakshmi worship service and devotional songs are chanted. Puja sponsorship usually begins at $51, but you can also just observe this ritual in a Hindu temple at no cost.

2. Order a Puja online: Thanks to the miracle of modern technology, Hindu priests at Indian temples bring your prayers to the goddess and bring the blessings of the Goddess to you when you order a puja online through www.saranam.com—an organization that places puja orders for people from around the world, and typically cost at around $59 (the prices are in rupees on their website, so clarify before you buy). You can request to be part of the worship services at Ashta Lakshmi Temple, in Chennai, Tamil Nadu; at MahaLakshmi Temple, in Mumbai, Maharashtra; or in one of 150 temples. They Fed Ex you a DVD of the worship service, as well as the prasad (dried flowers, red cum-cum, sandalwood ash, etc).

3. Admire her image: Like any goddess, Lakshmi likes to be noticed and appreciated! It is a long-standing Hindu tradition to evoke Lakshmi by focusing on her image or icon. The Hindu culture produces these images in huge quantities because they love to share their deities and make them available.

4. Pray to her: Since you may not get to attend a Hindu worship service to honor the goddess, it is important that you know Lakshmi can hear your prayers from wherever you may be. To evoke Her energy of good fortune, light a pink candle in Lakshmi's honor. Think for a moment about what good fortune means to you. Perhaps you may find that good fortune begins with a sense of peace and well-being within and has little to do with material goods or money. Or maybe you have a financial issue which, once resolved, will make you feel more fortunate.

   Although you can certainly pray to win the lottery, you may find more immediate results if you pray for whatever is needed to meet your financial obligations and whatever support you need to make your most heartfelt dreams come alive.

   It is the Hindu tradition to evoke the Lord of Obstacles, Ganesha, to clear the path of anything in the way of fortune. (Ganesha removes obstacles so Lakshmi can deliver fortune into your life.) It can be as simple as chanting or repeating "Om Ganesh" three times. Then ask the goddess for her help.

   Petition her as you would any deity: "Dear MahaLakshmi, please help me with ..." or, in Her spiritual presence, make a declaration: "I am ready to find the job (mate, apartment, car, etc.) that is perfect for me, now." In these challenging times, you can also pray to her for peace and well-being for all.

5. Call to her through the holiest blessing: "Sri Sukta" or "Lakshmi Sukta" is considered to be one of the most popular and "well-tested" among Lakshmi devotees. It's used in many forms of worship and uttered as a blessing during the building of Hindu temples. It is a composition of fifteen verses that have very specific intentions and guidelines for honoring Lakshmi. And a sixteenth verse contains the suggested method for attaining desires.

SRI SUKTA

This translation by J.L. Gupta for B.C. Butala Books embellishes the meanings of this ancient text in parentheses. Keep in mind it is quite ancient. It may make more sense when brought up to modern times—such as substituting requests for "cows" (unless you're a farmer) and "heirs" with prayers for a "new job" or a "beautiful home." I share it here with the original spelling (Laksmi) and punctuation.

> *O Jatavada! Bring Laksmi (the Goddess of Wealth) of golden color to me, (bring her to me) who is remover of sins, who is (resplendent) with her garlands of (lotuses of) gold and silver, who is the source of pleasure like the moon (for the universe) and who possesses a lot of (wealth) gold, etc. (1)*
>
> *O Jataveda! Bring me that Laksmi who will not ever desert me and by whose grace I may get gold, cows, horses and sons together with other descendants. (2)*
>
> *I invoke Goddess Sri (Laksmi) who has the cavalry before her and the chariots (carried by horses) in the middle, who delights the world by the resounding trumpet of elephants (attending on her). May she be graceful to me and reside at my place forever! (3)*
>
> *I invoke Sri, the blissful goddess, who is sweet-smiling, who lives in a hall of gold, who is full of compassion and drenched with it from the heart (due to the fact of being bathed by at-*

tending elephants or having risen from the milky ocean), who is resplendent at the seat of the lotus, is lotus-hued, and who bestows all pleasures to her devotees. (4)

I take refuge in Sri who is the effulgent one like the moon, who shines with the fame of herself, who is adored by the Gods like Indra, etc. Who is benevolent in offering gifts, who dwells in the middle of the lotus, who protects all (her devotees). May the poverty be removed from my end, (and for that) I invoke you, O Goddess Laksmi. (5)

O (Laksmi) of sun-like lustre! The Tree of the name Bilva was produced by your penance. May the fruits of that tree remove all our ignorance, distresses and other extrinsic things by (our) penance. (6)

O Mother Laksmi! May the Gods like Indra, Kubera (friend of Mahadeva) come to me together with fame and gems. (Here the fame is Sati, the daughter of Daksa, and the gems are the friends of Kubera like Manibhadra) I am born in this world and may you (Kubera) give me fame and plenty for wealth. (7)

I destroy the poverty (Alakshmi) which is the cause of hunger and thirst, which is the elder sister of Lasksmi, and which is impure. O Goddess, please get the paucity of wealth from my abode obliterated and all the hurdles in the way of the acquisition of wealth be removed. (8)

I invoke Sri, who is to be gotten by offering fragrant flowers, who is unassailable, who has abundance of crops and wealth and cattle, and who is supreme of all beings. (9)

O, Laksmi! May we realize all the wishes of our hearts and willingness, the truth of our words, the wealth of cattle (milk, curd, etc.) and forms of food. May Goddess bring me fame and wealth too. (10)

O Kardama! Come dwell in me. Make Sri, who is the Universal Mother and who is adorned with a garland of lotuses, dwell in my family. (11)

(It is said that Lord Varuna produces oily substances, i.e., beautiful things) (The beauty in substances is known as Laksmi. She has three sons—Kardam, Ciklita and Sruti. Here Ciklita is prayed: O Ciklita (son of Laksmi)! Come to dwell in my house, and, not only you but make your mother (also Mother of The Universe), Laksmi, also live in my abode. (12)

O Lord Agni, (God of Fire)! Bring to me Laksmi, who is very kind, who has elephants around her pouring water on her (for her bath), who is the goal of sacrificial rites, who is tawny-hued, who is decked with a garland of lotuses, who is lustrous like the moon and thus enlightening the living beings and also possessed of plenty of wealth. (13)

O Jataveda! Bring to me Mother Laksmi, who is always compassionate to her devotees, who punishes the wicked ones, who is golden (exquisitely beautiful) color, who puts on garland of gold, who is wealth (herself), and who makes the whole world illumine like the sun. (14)

O Jataveda! Bring to me Laksmi who will never leave me and by whose grace I may get plenty of gold, prosperity, cows, horses, servants and other descendants. (15)

One who aspires for the attainment of Laksmi, should regularly, in a sanctified and determined way, offer the cow-ghee in oblation and recite all the 15 verses of Srisuktam. (16)

—Sri Suktam, translated by Jawaharlal Gupta, published by B.C. Butal

CLOSING THOUGHTS

In these challenging times, you can also pray to Lakshmi for peace and well-being for all. Good fortune on all levels is her domain. Not only is she is a *Creatress* who can help us all rebuild our lives and our consciousness with the mindset of good fortune and love, She is a nurturer and *protectress*, a Mother of the Universe.

NEXT LESSON

Meet Sekhmet, Ancient Egyptian
Goddess of War and Healing

Lesson Ten

MEET SEKHMET, ANCIENT EGYPTIAN GODDESS OF WAR & HEALING

"Sekhmet is the scorching, destructive power of the sun.
She is strong, mighty, violent—she is no gentle pussycat.
Sekhment is the power of the sun at its height."
— Anthon Veggi and Alison Davidson, from The Book of Doors

MINDSET PREPARATION

Breathe deeply and exhale ... Arch your back and stretch your arms overhead. Clasp your hands together and use your pointer fingers to point toward the heavens (think yoga warrior one pose). Begin this lesson with this affirmation:

"I am the power in my world."

If so moved, you might even get out of your chair and do a female super hero warrior pose: Back errect, hands on hips and eyes confidently gazing forward and upward.

The ancient Egyptians experienced Sekhmet as the Mighty One. They sought to avoid her wrath and to honor her special powers.

THOUGHTS TO CONSIDER

Who would have thought that "bad energy" and "negative vibes" would be the modern day enemy of people attempting to travel a spiritual path (and any path)?

Getting zapped by other people's energetic reactions (e.g., anger, rage, upset, and disappointment) can pack a punch as it travels through the ethers! The general "bad news" consciousness of our culture is a very real dilemma. Especially for those of us who are sensitive to "feelings about things" or "vibes."

BAD VIBRATIONS

How can you tell if you are affected by negative energy? It may be subtle, but it can drag down your whole day.

You may be talking to someone and feel a twinge of nausea in your stomach, or you may pass someone on the street and feel your heart pound faster with fear. Sometimes in the course of daily life, your eyes will link with someone who simply gives you the heebie-jeebies. Or you may just feel vaguely rattled by indescribable discomfort around certain people or in certain places.

I believe that very sensitive people can feel it when people close to them think ill of them or talk about them behind their backs; some people can even feel the sting of other people's unexpressed jealousies and envy.

Then there are those people who are classic energy drainers and happiness thieves. My friend Dr. Judith Orloff, MD, calls them, "Energy Vampires." They suck good energy from a room and deplete people around them.

It is important to learn to read energy and trust your intuition about it and also screen the vibes that come your way.

Disruptive, unpleasant or draining energies around us can distract us from spiritual pursuits. They can even make us want to recoil from life and sometimes forget our dreams and goals. They can tire us and make us feel wiped out.

When we get a sense that something is not quite right, we have to learn to be brave and do what we must to energetically protect ourselves. Part of it is to honor ourselves enough to be unwilling to be hurt by the negative and nasty vibes perpetuated by other people—those we know, and those we don't know.

If an interaction or experience doesn't feel good, if it makes you cranky, if it gives you the creeps, if it makes you want to cry, you may be experiencing a *negative energy exchange* with someone. And you have the right to end it right there.

SEKHMET CAN HELP YOU SUMMON YOUR COURAGE AND TENACITY

Sekhmet brings some fiery goddess power to any situation. She can help you stand firmly in your power when you need to energetically defend or protect yourself. Although it is your responsibility always to work with energy in a way that "harms none"—her fiery rays can propel others in the opposite direction. Although under the lion can live a pussycat, she represents serious power, psychic force, and passion. Try to imagine her as a lioness who helps guard you against situations that are harmful to your emotional, mental and spiritual health. This is her way of helping you heal.

SEKHMET IS THE LION-HEADED GODDESS OF EGYPT.

As one of the most ancient goddesses known to the human race, her age carries great clout; she is called "Lady of the Place of the Beginning of Time." She is a war and healing goddess who is a force to be reckoned with. She is depicted in countless ancient statues and reliefs with a slim female body and a lion head; she symbolizes the protective energy of the lioness. Fierce, yet focused, she is not known for random slaughter but for specifically protecting her turf, her interests and anything she loves.

As protectress of Divine Order, Sekhmet safeguards the gods against evil, and many believe she protects mortals as well. Unlikely to initiate an unprovoked attack, she responds to aggression in a New York minute, with the agility of a lioness defending her young. She represents the cleansing fire that brings energy into form. In addition to her ferocity, Sekhmet's strong magical powers caused her to be highly regarded as a healer. The flail in her left hand attracts celestial energy. Although she has seen bloody battle, her powers are dedicated to righteous ends, protection, and the healing of difficult situations.

THE MYTH OF HER RATH

Sekhmet is consort/sister of Ptah (the Craft God and protector of artisan), and the daughter of Ra (the Sun God); she is also sometimes referred to as "Eye of Ra," because he sent his eye, in the form of his lioness daughter, to earth to be the watchful presence and the power that protects the good and annihilates the wicked. This reference most notably comes from her role in *The Myth of the Destruction of Mankind,* a scenario that recounts the beginning of time when humans conspired to overthrow the gods, making Ra mighty angry. Ra called together a council of deities to come up with clever ways to deal with the wayward humans; they voted that Sekhmet would manifest on earth to punish the humans who conspired evil plots, saying, "Let thine eye go forth against these rebels. When it cometh down from heaven, no human eye can be raised against it."

Sekhmet, being passionate, went full tilt and would have devoured all humanity if the gods didn't decide to intervene and save mankind from destruction. To sway Sekhmet from anymore butt-kicking of insurgents, Ra covered the ground with a red-dyed beer to make her believe she had spilled the blood of all evil humans. Fooled by the color, she sipped the liquid, became drunk and fell asleep, sparing mankind. It is said that she was taken to another part of Egypt to chill out and it was there that she transformed into her gentler, more playful feline aspect, Bast, the cat goddess. (Although Bast is a goddess unto herself, she is also looked upon by some as the gentler side of the lioness goddess.)

THIS WEEK, TRY THIS

Sekhmet can be fierce, and she is tempestuous, fiery, and magical in nature, so when you evoke her, make sure you are grounded and centered, and that your intentions are clear. Call on her to help you develop bravery in the face of perceived danger and courage to take care of yourself and make your own well-being your first priority.

1. See her for yourself: Can you get to a museum that has an Egyptian collection? Please do if at all possible! Sekhmet offers the unique advantage of direct experience via her image and statuary, which are present in most Egyptian antiquity collections. In New York, you can stand within inches of a powerful bust of the goddess in the Brooklyn Museum and you can walk past and hang out around an array of seven identical, life-sized statues that stand in the Egypt atrium at the American Museum of Art. Her energy is clearly broadcast from all. Very powerful connections can be made with her through connecting with her antiquities.
2. Keep a picture of Sekhmet or a lioness at your office or home: Imagine your office is the lioness lair and place energetic shields around you to repel energies of anyone who would endanger your well-being or seek to off balance you. You can easily buy or download her image. She is featured in many Egyptian wall reliefs that exist today in ancient temples and is featured in hundreds of ancient statues and busts. Gaze at her whenever you feel vulnerable, trust you can conjure the lioness within, at any time, and that she will guard over you and let no one hurt you.
3. Purchase a Sekhmet statue. Keep her golden form right on your desk to watch over you while you work. These are very powerful and easy to obtain on Amazon or eBay.

4. Call to the lioness within. One of the most dynamic aspects of Sekhmet is her physical presence and prowess. She's fierce, a physical force to be reckoned with. In this form, she was more in touch with her male energy, then her female side. This is something we women all need to do from time to time.

Like many goddesses, there are hundreds of names associated with Sekhmet. In *The Goddess Sekhmet: The Way of The Five Bodies*, author Robert Masters suggests that speaking the names of the goddess while gazing at her image offers a powerful experience of, "The reality known as Sekhmet." Masters says that savoring the names will activate the Goddess within. I have culled twenty-six versions of her name from Masters' book to help you give this a try. (He gave me permission to share them with readers about 20 years ago when I was working on my first Goddess book.) As a wild goddess with the reputation for being ruthless and appropriately aggressive in the face of battle for that which is right, Sekhmet is not a goddess to call upon for petty differences between friends. Call to her only when you truly need to lean into her power to help you create an energetic boundary that protects you, and harms none.

Center yourself, light an orange or gold candle to represent the bright sun, and quietly speak these twenty-six names—or just the ones that call to you.

If you really get into it, you can chant or sing them, and feel her presence filling you and the space all around you.

NAMES OF SEKHMET

1. Awakener
2. Lady of Enchantments
3. Opener of Ways
4. Lady Of Transformations
5. Enrapturing One

6. Satisfier Of Desires
7. Victorious One In Battles
8. Overcomer Of All Enemies
9. Ruler Of Lions
10. Complete One
11. Sublime One
12. Empowerer
13. Great One of Healing
14. Unrivaled And Invincible One
15. The Source
16. She Whose Opportunity Escapeth Her Not
17. Powerful Of Heart
18. Lady Of All Powers
19. Incomparable One
20. Most Beautiful
21. Most Strong
22. Protectress Of The Divine Order
23. The Beautiful Light
24. Warrior Goddess
25. Unwavering, Loyal One
26. Beloved Sekhmet

CLOSING THOUGHTS

It is time to create wholeness within ourselves but, to put it simply, it is time to listen to our Divine Mother. See if she speaks to you, shows you images or shares wisdom with you in daily life.

NEXT LESSON

Meet Kali, the Hindu Black Mother Goddess

Lesson Eleven

MEET KALI, THE HINDU BLACK MOTHER GODDESS

"Kali represents the entire physical plane. She is the drama, tragedy, humor, and sorrow of life. She is the brother, father, sister, mother, lover, and friend. She is the fiend, monster, beast, and brute ... The full and seductive, terrible and wonderful earth mother always has something to offer." **—Robert M. Pirsig, Zen and the Art of Motorcycle Maintenance**

MINDSET PREPARATION

Breathe into your heart center to a count of four:

1, 2, 3, 4

Hold the breath for a count of eight:

1, 2, 3, 4, 5, 6, 7, 8

As you exhale, breathe out all that is dark and lonely within you. Breathe in light, breathe out darkness.

Repeat until you feel space in your heart center. Now begin today's lesson with an open heart and mind.

Kali is the Dark Mother of the Hindu tradition. She slays ignorance and the ego. She shines a light on dysfunction so you can heal it.

THOUGHTS TO CONSIDER

Many of our lives are shaped around dysfunctional family backgrounds, and we tend to try to disassociate from them, as we get older. It's a good idea to grow up and leave the past behind.

But if we don't examine the pain of the past and make an attempt to heal it, we will drag it with us through life ... and hungry ghosts of the past will plague us.

We tend to think of ghosts as "supernatural" beings who haunt and taunt us and somehow chain us to our fears. They make a racket, loom around us in a threatening way and manifest in a manner so frightening we feel we must do anything to quiet them down. Our very survival would seem to be at stake. But what is scariest and most unsettling about a ghost is we don't really know what it is. Is it a lost spirit or fiendish monster of our own minds? All we know is that there is a presence that somehow holds a power over us; we may not even know why. There are many parallels to be drawn between a Hollywood poltergeist and the family members and people of the past with whom you share unresolved issues. Both can haunt you.

Whether flesh and blood living relatives, the deceased or those who have moved on from our lives, hungry ghosts can insidiously haunt our daily lives—until we make a decision to set them free. It's a human impulse to run from the darkness. Yet, when you understand the truth about the shadow cast by hungry ghosts, you won't feel the need to run. Learn what they have come to teach by making all that racket in your life and then, say, "Boo."

GODDESS KALI, THE BLACK MOTHER

Kali, also known as Kali Ma and the Black Mother, is the powerful Hindu Goddess who is in charge of darkness, death, and regeneration. Many people fear her because she is so fearsome looking, but Hindus love and adore her as their great mother goddess and they see her as a manifestation of power that is fierce and potent. She is Shakti (female energy) incarnate and the manifestation of primordial power. While she is the consort of the great Lord Shiva, she is also seen dancing wildly, with his form beneath her feet. They are partners in darkness, and in dancing the dance of death and regeneration. She brings life and death; she is regeneration and rebirth.

THE MYTHOLOGY OF KALI

Her haunts are cremation grounds where she takes life, and then recycles it into a new life. She beheads true evil and darkness, and she swallows the ego so that it cannot give us problems. She eats pain, despair, and the secret shadows of our lives. She wipes out oddball beliefs, worn out thoughts and constructs that no longer serve us. She is a wild goddess. She is black and wears a garland of skulls around her neck. She has four arms; a symbol of domination over the world. In one hand she holds a head dripping blood, in the other three she wields various weapons. One of her hands removes fear and another grants bliss. Her tongue is sticking out and her eyes look wild.

THIS WEEK, TRY THIS

1. Make a list of issues with family and friends you have been avoiding with the intention of asking Kali to help heal these situations so all parties can evolve and move past them.
2. Recognize which situations seem hopeless and make you feel powerless. Embrace these.
3. Search and download an image of the goddess and place it in your living room. Create a little shrine with a photo or photos of the loved ones you feel conflicted about.
4. Every day, for thirty days, stand in front of this shrine and pray that disagreements and painful situations be healed for the highest good of all involved.

Praise Kali and pray to her directly. Thank her, in advance, for her help. Hindus praise Mother Kali in many ways. She is considered the great, all-powerful Devi, the dark destructress and the rebirther of the new you. Call to her in this Shloka, or prayer to Devi (Sanskrit for Goddess) from Hindunet.com.

O mother, who is present everywhere, who is embodiment of Universal Mother,
O mother, who is present everywhere, who is embodiment of Power and Energy,
O mother, who is present everywhere, who is embodiment of Peace,
I bow to thee, I bow to thee, I bow to thee.

CLOSING THOUGHTS

Kali is only dark from a distance. Many people fear the dark mother. Recognize that she is not so scary, and our own dark sides are not as scary as we may think or imagine. This poem by Hindu Saint Ramakrishna Paramhansa (1836-86) explains the Black Mother looks fierce before you get to know her, but she's not so intimidating on closer examination.

Is Kali, my Divine Mother, of a black complexion?
She appears black because She is viewed from a distance;
but when intimately known She is no longer so.
The sky appears blue at a distance, but look at it close by
and you will find that it has no colour.
The water of the ocean looks blue at a distance,
but when you go near and take it in your hand,
you find that it is colourless.

NEXT LESSON

Meet Pachamama, Peruvian Earth Goddess

Lesson Twelve

MEET PACHAMAMA, PERUVIAN EARTH GODDESS

We all come from the Goddess,
— ©**Zsuzsanna Budapest**

MINDSET PREPARATION

Take a few moments to relax and breathe deeply, exhale ...

In your mind's eye, visualize the trees and vegetation in and around your home and in your community. Feel appreciation for their contribution to the health and beauty of your neighborhood and life.

Expand the vision to the entire planet; feel your connectedness to all things.

Send love, light, and gratitude to Mother Earth for ALL She provides to us: food, water, air, life and everything else.

THOUGHTS TO CONSIDER

To truly connect with the Goddess, we have to really *get* that we are part of *Her* and *She* is part of us—every day. She is the earth we stand on, and the elements of our common being. She is not separate from us. She is the one who gives life. It is to her we shall all return at the end of our days when our bodies become part of her body, or our ashes are scattered into the breath of her winds.

GRATITUDE FOR MOTHER EARTH

Appreciating Her and all her glories is a powerful way to understand the true nature of our connection to the Divine Female.

It can be as simple as going out into the backyard or enjoying a moment in nature, anywhere. Smell the flowers. Appreciate the trees. Enjoy the sound of a babbling brook. Revel in the scent and sight of the sea. Gaze at a green meadow or mountain peak.

She is in the small graces of everyday life—the squirrel who scoots along the telephone pole, the bee that pollinates the flowers. She guides the cycles of our being.

Just stand on Her earth beneath Her full moon ... and feel her awesome power.

We live and breathe Her being each day of our lives. While we can find Her in the thousands of names, faces, and stories about the Divine Feminine from all cultures, we can find Her, quite simply, in our everyday existence on earth.

You do not need an intermediary (like a clergy person or church). She is truly a temple unto herself.

EARTH IS HER BODY

Here is a chant that is often sung when people gather in groups to honor the goddess. Typically, it is chanted for many rounds, over and over, until you feel the energy of the Goddess coursing through you. You can sing it any time!

"Earth is my body,
Water my blood.
Air is my breath,
And Fire my spirit."

THE PERSONIFICATION OF MOTHER EARTH

One of the ways we have come to deify the earth is to name her. The ancients called her *Magna Mother* and *Terra*. The Greeks called her *Gaia*. Many call her, still, *the Great Mother*. And of course, we know her as *Mother Earth*, *Mother Nature* or *Mom Nature*.

She also comes to life in the Incan legends and the modern day worship of *Pachamama*, who is seen as earth and all Her attributes, and Mother of all things.

PACHAMAMA, PERUVIAN EARTH GODDESS

Pachamama is the Incan Earth Mother. To this day, she is worshipped by indigenous people of Peru, Bolivia, and Chile, who honor her as they till the earth, and harvest her bounty. She remains the object of a cult all over the Andean mountains where people (especially farmers and those who work with the earth) make her offerings of coca leaf and chicha beer and pray to her on all major agricultural occasions.

She is a full-bodied earth goddess, primordial and ever-present. She is said to live inside the earth and is a companion to women, and she is our sacred earth home. Indigenous people believe her feminine spirit dwells among them and in the land and they see her as the First Mother. As a "Divine Earth Mother," she is often mentioned in the same breath as Gaia and Mother Earth. In modern images, she is pictured as a wise woman or grandmother whose face is lined with character and whose eyes radiate love.

THE MYTHOLOGY OF PACHAMAMA

In Inca mythology, Mama Pacha—or Pachamama—was the fertility goddess who presided over planting and harvesting. It was to her that earthquakes and earth changes were attributed. In her early incarnations, she was a dragoness; she was connected to her husband/consort Pacha Camac, also known as "Creator of the world." She was worshiped in Chile, Bolivia, and Peru. After the Spanish conquest of Peru, the Christian priests burned many of the records of Inca culture.

Indigenous women adapted icons of the Virgin Mary as their spiritual mother but to them, she represented the energy of Pachamama in physical form. Peru remains an ancient place where the ancient wisdom and ways have survived. One Andean mystery school says the feminine spirit of Pachamama lives specifically in the Andes, and is precisely anchored in the triangle that is Machu Picchu, the Sacred Valley of the Incas, and Lake Titicaca. It is this triangle depicted in ancient cave art and tribal drawings that has always symbolized the emergence of the Divine Feminine.

THIS WEEK, TRY THIS

I found this quote by James E. Tarvid on a shamanic website years ago. Let this insight inspire you.

> *"Pachamama is the Andean Goddess Mother Earth. Unlike European notions of God, She is not apart from Earth but the very Earth that gave us life, sustains us and will receive us at the end. There are three rules of Pachamama. First, whenever we are hungry and thirsty, we should remember that Pachamama is hungry and thirsty too; and we should take care of her first. Second, there are times when Pachamama does not want to be touched and we should leave her alone. Third, there are times when Pachamama is sad and wants to be consoled; we should bring her flowers."*

1. Think of ways (practical and spiritual) that you can give back to the Mother by honoring the earth.
    - Do a reality check and discover what your carbon footprint is and look for ways to reduce it.
    - Make a list of ways you can include a "greener" ap-

proach to life. It could be as simple as making more of an effort to recycle, or stepping outside to water your plants. It may be using environmentally friendly cleaning products or doing one less load of laundry. Whatever you choose to do, or sacrifice, make it an offering to the Mother.

2. Practice gratitude. It is human nature to always want more and want to do better. We forget sometimes and we dishonor or ignore her. And we get mad at Mom Nature when she brings destruction or demands we pay attention to her by throwing a hissy fit in the form of a hurricane, tidal wave, or earthquake (Yes, those too are a part of the Great Mother). She will forgive us. We must also forgive her and begin to imbue our lives with an appreciation and gratitude. Gratitude is not only a spiritually correct quality; it is empowering and brings more of the same.
   - When you awake in the morning, make a list of five or ten things you would like to experience in your day. Thank The Mother, in advance, for supporting you in achieving them.
   - As you get ready for bed, review the good things that happened and make note of them—even if these are not part of your morning choices. Make a list of at least five things to be thankful for each night. Just like the classic childhood prayer of thanks, go to bed at night with a prayer of gratitude on your lips and in your heart.
3. Gratitude fuels your connection with the Divine. Here are some very simple ideas to work with. And remember, when you honor the Great Mother or Mother Earth, you are honoring God, Goddess and all there is and you are honoring yourself.

- When you take a meal, say a prayer of thanks to the Goddess for providing such bounty.
- When you get your paycheck every week or receive a check for work you have done, say thanks to the Goddess for empowering your financial life.
- When you receive a gift of any kind, say thanks to the Goddess for gifting you.
- Whenever someone does something nice or offers you kindness, say thanks to the Goddess and in her name offer a nice gesture or kindness to another.
- When you catch your reflection in the mirror, say thanks for the ability to see yourself so clearly and make fortunate and positive choices in life.
- Practice these concepts. Get into the *gratitude groove*. Expressing gratitude to the Mother for all the little things is a way of staying connected with her throughout your day!

4. Buy a poster or download a photo of Mother Earth and put it somewhere you can appreciate Her every day.
    - Just Google "photo of earth," find a photo and print it.
    - Whenever you gaze at the photo say, "Thank you."

CLOSING THOUGHTS

Spend the time between this week and the next appreciating and observing nature. Look for the Goddess in everyday sites—trees, flowers, your backyard, a park, a lake, the moon, a mountain. The earth mother dwells in all of life.

NEXT LESSON

Quick Ways to Connect with the Goddesses

Lesson Thirteen

QUICK WAYS TO INVOKE THE GODDESS

"The image of the Goddess inspires women to see ourselves as divine, our bodies as sacred, the changing phases of our lives as holy, our aggression as healthy, our anger as purifying, and our power to nurture and create, but also to limit and destroy when necessary, as the very force that sustains all life. Through the Goddess we can discover our strength, enlighten our minds, own our bodies, and celebrate our emotions. We can move beyond narrow, constricting roles and become whole." —**Starhawk**

THESE EIGHT WELL-KNOWN GODDESSES ARE sought out for their special qualities—such as beauty, abundance, healing, and inspiration. Here are some quick ways to connect with the energy and qualities of these famous divine females.

VENUS: LOVE YOURSELF

Venus, the Roman goddess of love, beauty, and sexuality, is one of the most famous goddesses on the planet, and also has her own planet—Venus, planet of poetry, music, pleasure and love. Her name is synonymous with all that is feminine, and with love and passion. She is reputed for her sizzling sexuality, her thorough enjoyment of her own exploits and for a complete and utter appreciation of self.

Special qualities: Inspiring love, romance, and self-love

Evoke Her: Create special vows of love—to yourself, such as: I promise to treat myself well and offer the same kindness, love, and compassion to myself as I do others. I will always honor and cherish myself. Speak them as you look into a mirror.

Affirmation: "I am worthy of love."

KUAN YIN: FIND COMPASSION

Kuan Yin is the Chinese Buddhist goddess of compassion, mercy, and healing. She is the "Compassionate Saviouress" worshiped for centuries throughout China, Japan, Korea, and South East Asia. Known also as Quan Yin and Guan Shih Yin, she is the patron and protector of women, children, sailors, artisans, and those who are imprisoned. Her name is translated as the being who hears the cries of the world. She is a Bodhisattva, which in Buddhism is a human being who has completed all Karma and reached enlightenment.

Special qualities: Compassionate, caring, loving kindness, healing human pain.

Evoke her: Chant to her any time. Her powers and gifts can be invoked by calling her name or chanting the famous "Mani": Om Mani Padme Hum (Oh-m mah'-nee pahd'-may hoom).

Affirmation: "I forgive myself for any ways in which I have disappointed myself or others. And I forgive others for disappointing me."

BRIGID: FIND YOUR INSPIRATION

Brigid is the Celtic Triple Goddess known as keeper of the sacred fire. Her name means "exalted one" and she is sometimes referred to a "bride." Goddess of poets, blacksmiths, brides, and childbirth, she watched over the hearth, fire, fertility, creativity, healing. As a triple goddess, she represents the three aspects of the divine feminine and three stages of a woman's life—maiden, mother, and wise woman—all in one.

Special Qualities: Empowering self-expression and bringing new ideas into the world and giving them life.

Evoke her: The ancients lit a candle in her honor for nineteen days and it was said on the twentieth the goddess appeared. Light a candle and visualize that whatever you are trying to create—or work through—is completed.

Affirmation: "Inspiration fills me. My creativity flows easily."

ISIS: HEAL YOUR RELATIONSHIPS

Isis is one of the earliest and most important goddesses in ancient Egypt. Her worship was a major part of Egyptian culture just over two thousand years ago; her image abounds on the walls of Egyptian temples and tombs and in museums around the world. Known as a healer, physician, enchantress, magician, patron of women in childbirth, mother, and devoted wife she is referred to as Goddess of Ten Thousand Names. In her eternal relationship with her beloved Osiris—her brother, husband, lover, and co-ruler—she shared the same soul. When he was killed, Osiris became King of the Underworld and Isis the Queen of Heaven, together they rule still.

Special qualities: Commitment in the long haul, devotion, and keeping relationships sacred.

Evoke her: Her image lives on in ancient temples and relief's, and she is often seen carrying an ankh, symbol of eternal life. Buy an ankh necklace or download an image and place it somewhere you can see if daily.

Affirmation: "I am in you. You are in me."

THE MUSES: HONOR FEMALE FRIENDSHIP

The muses, the Greek deities who presided over the arts, are among the most familiar mythical women. Although the numbers varied from region to region, the classical period in Greece established them as nine. Each had their own distinct area of expertise: Calliope was Muse of epic poetry; Clio, history; Erato, the lyre; Euterpe, the flute; Polyhymnia, hymns and mime; Terpsichore, dance; Thalia, comedy; Urania, astronomy; and their mother, Mnemosyne, Muse of tragedy and memory. Hesiod suggested that the Muses were the ultimate party girls of Greece, "their hearts set upon song and their spirit is free from care." Taking great pleasure in merriment, good food, and celebration, they helped mortals lighten up and allow their creativity to flow.

Special qualities: Inspiration for creative endeavors, joyful self-expression, and sacred sisterhood.

Evoke them: Call together your favorite women, gather in a sacred circle, make declarations about your creative endeavors, and promise to support each other in fulfilling your dreams.

Affirmation: "My life is filled with muses who inspire me in all ways."

GREEN TARA: FEEL PROTECTED

Tara is the much-loved Tibetan Buddhist mother goddess. Monks and devotees around the world chant and evoke her energies daily, calling upon her for everything from world peace, to inner peace, and protection. Tara is worshiped in both mild and wild forms and exists in a rainbow of colors based on various attributes. As Green Tara, she is a goddess of action, great strength and special protective powers who wards off evil and shields you from spiritual harm.

Special powers: Deflecting negative energy, overcoming danger, quelling fear and anxiety.

Evoke her: Light incense and chant her mantra. "Om Tare Tuttare Ture Soha," (Ah-um Tah-ray Too-tah-ray Too-ray So-hah)

Affirmation: "I am safe and sound in the arms of the Mother."

WHITE BUFFALO CALF WOMAN: CREATE PEACE

White Buffalo Calf Woman is a Native American spirit woman considered a holy woman-savior who came here to give instructions for living the sacred life to "The People." In Native American Culture, she is credited with helping the Lakota and Sioux establish rituals and a sacred social life that would bring them closer to Great Spirit, the Great Mother and one another, as well as teaching them how to perpetuate peace and honesty in their world.

Special qualities: Activating your ability to build a peaceful community and spread peace.

Evoke her: Focus on peace, every day. Take a "peace break" in lieu of a coffee break, and softly or silently chant: Peace to my right. Peace to my left. Peace in front of me. Peace in back of me. Peace above me. Peace below me. Peace within me. Peace all about. Peace abounds. Peace is mine.

Affirmation: "I radiate peace everywhere I go."

THE GREAT GODDESS: CONNECTING TO THE FEMININE

The Great Goddess is the Great Mother of all things. The earliest artifacts of goddess worship date back over 40,000 years and many believe that the first God worshipped was a woman She is the earth we stand on, the air we breathe, the fire we cook with, the waters of life that sustain us and the spirit that lives inside us and all around us. She can be found in the history, mythology, sacred texts, spiritual practices and folklore of every culture. In the beginning, she was Inanna, Ishtar, Isis, Astarte, and Gaia and in modern times she's come to be known as Mother Nature.

Special qualities: Connects you to all ancestors and all women, unconditional love, and nurturing.

Evoke her: Spend time in nature. A walk in the park, a talk on the patio, a hike up a mountain, a moment gazing at the full moon, a swim in the sea will all bring you closer.

Affirmation: "We are all the children of the Great Mother."

NEXT LESSON:

Goddess Chants and Prayers
Prepare to enter the Temple of the Goddess in your heart and mind and connect to the Mother through prayer

Lesson Fourteen

GODDESS PRAYERS AND CHANTS

YOU MAY BE MOST FAMILIAR for prayers to God and the male divine. But many of the world's cultures express worship to the Goddess in chant and prayer. Here is a sampling of goddess chants and prayers, old and new, to help you connect with the Divine Feminine.

The oldest religions, such as Hinduism and Buddhism, still offer ancient prayers and chants to the Goddess. Over time, new ones have been created to honor Goddess spirituality. Here is a collection of old and new prayers and chants to the Goddess.

Sit. Quiet yourself. Light a candle in your heart. And pray to the Goddess to help you with your challenges of the moment. Express gratitude in advance for all the help She will bring your way.

PRAYER FOR RENEWAL

Divine Mother of All there is, whose essence Lies within us all and in all things.
Please fill this place with your sacred light and presence.
Please protect me and heal me.
Please bring me to wholeness and wisdom.
Make this a day of fresh starts, new beginnings.
Melt all obstacles in my path—gently, gracefully, lovingly.
Reconnect me to my highest self. Awaken me to what I need

to know next.
Let my higher self select and connect with the divine energy that is right for me, right now.
May I be uplifted and empowered by your Love.
So be it and so it is.
–Rev. Laurie Sue Brockway

PRAYER TO THE GODDESS OF THE NEW DAWN

Dearest Aurora, Goddess of dawn,
Please bring illumination in early morn.
As you awaken at your twilight hour,
Let me feel your energy and power.
–Rev. Laurie Sue Brockway

PRAYER FOR OVEREATERS

Dear Mother, Father, Great Spirit of All There Is,
Please Guide us to eating good, nutritious food.
Protect us from unhealthy eating.
Save us from food that makes us fat.
Remove the spell of carbohydrates, sugar
and additives from our diets. And keep addictive munchies and crunchies out of reach.
Strengthen us. Let us feed on Love.
And please, also, make sure we have all the protein and nutrition we need, to balance blood sugar and life.
Feed me your manna from heaven.
And fill us with the low-carb, low-calorie, high protein bounty of the earth.
And so it is. Thank you!!!!
— Rev. Laurie Sue Brockway

PRAYER TO SOPHIA, THE GODDESS OF WISDOM

May the spirit of wisdom
Shine her light in my consciousness
And connect me to my truth
And my highest mind,
Now and always.
— Rev. Laurie Sue Brockway

PRAYER TO BRIGID, GODDESS OF INSPIRATION

Brigid of the golden flame and fiery inspiration, I welcome you. Please bring me the inspiration and motivation I need to ________ [fill your need].
On this day I pray that this sacred flame lead me to your light. Amen.
— Rev. Laurie Sue Brockway

THE LADY'S PRAYER

Divine Mother,
Whose Essence lies in all,
Goddess is Thy name.
Thy blessings come,
My will be done
In accordance with Your Divine Plan.
Give me this day, the wisdom to co-create
For the good of all, with harm to none.
And bless me with compassion for those I do not understand,
As well as those who do not understand me.
Illuminate Thy path of Truth before me,
And awaken me from my own illusions.
For Thou art the Universe, Love and Spirit within.
So be it! Blessed Be.
— Connia Silver,

Spiritual writer and educator on intuitive skills and Goddess mysteries

PROTECTION OF THE GODDESS CHANT

May the arms of the great mother ever surround me.
May the arms of the great mother ever surround me.
I invoke the protection of divine mother's embrace.
I invoke the protection of divine mother's grace.
— Lisa Thiel © 1992 Lisa Thiel, from Lady of the Lake used with permission.

PRAISE AND PRAYER TO HINDU GODDESS KALI

O mother, who is present everywhere, who is embodiment of Universal Mother,
O mother, who is present everywhere, who is embodiment of Power and Energy,
O mother, who is present everywhere, who is embodiment of Peace,
I bow to thee, I bow to thee, I bow to thee.
— Classic prayer,
from Hindunet.com

SABBATH PRAYER TO THE HEBREW GODDESS, SHEKHINA

The Sun on the treetops is no longer seen.
Come gather to welcome the Sabbath, our Queen.
Behold her descending. The holy. The blessed
And with Her the angels of peace and rest.
Draw near, and here abide.
Draw near, draw near, O Sabbath Bride.
Peace also to you, you angels of peace.
— Rabbi Joseph Gelberman and Rabbi Roger Ross
©The New Synagogue prayer book

WE ALL COME FROM THE GODDESS CHANT

We all come from the Goddess
And to her we shall return,
Like a drop of rain
Flowing from the ocean.
— © Z. Budapest
Classic goddess chant used in sacred circles

EARTH MY BODY CHANT

Earth my body
Water my blood
Air my breath
And Fire my spirit
— Classic Goddess Chant,
Author Unknown

ANCIENT MOTHER CHANT

Ancient Mother, I Hear You Calling
Ancient Mother, I Hear Your Song
Ancient Mother, I Hear Your Laughter
Ancient Mother, I Taste Your Tears
— Classic Goddess Chant, Author Unknown

THE EARTH IS OUR MOTHER CHANT

The earth is our mother
We must take care of her
The earth is our mother
We must take care of her
—Lakota Chant,

MAY THE CIRCLE BE OPEN CHANT

May the circle be open but unbroken
May the peace of the Goddess be ever in your heart
Merry meet, and merry part,
And merry meet again
— Classic Chant,

BLESSING FROM HER

May the blessing of God go before you.
May Her peace and grace abound.
May her spirit live within you.
May her love wrap you 'round.
May her blessing remain with you always.
May you walk on holy ground.
— Miriam Therese Winter, from Life Prayers, (HarperCollins, 1998)

Lesson Fifteen

GODDESS QUIZ

NOW THAT YOU'VE HAD MANY lessons about the Divine Feminine, and have studied on your own, you can see that goddesses pervade our culture more than we even realize. You probably know about some of them from history class or movies. They are in mythology, religious legends, history, folktales, and famous museums. Mythological goddess names are on everything from menus to running shoes. But how much do we know about the world's many interpretations of the Divine Feminine?

Have fun seeing if you can match the symbols and stories with the famous goddess legend.

A. Julius Caesar caused a scandal in Rome when he built a statue of Queen Cleopatra, dressed as her patron Egyptian Goddess, Isis, in a temple devoted to which Roman Goddess?

1. Venus
2. Juneo
3. Ceres
4. Diana

B. In the story of Demeter and Persephone, Hades strikes a deal that Persephone stay with him in the underworld for six months of the year, allowing her to stay with her mother for the other six months, based on the number of

seeds she's ingested. What kind of seeds did Persephone eat?

1. Pumpkin
2. Sesame
3. Sunflower
4. Pomegranate

C. **Kuan Yin, the Buddhist Bodhisattva of Compassion, is known as a deity who heals the suffering of the world and especially one who aids women. She is often seen in sculptures, and sacred art, holding a vase. What does it represent?**

1. A vessel to hold and pour out the tears of the world
2. Milk for the babies of the world
3. Love potion
4. Amrita

D. **Amaterasu is the Japanese Sun Goddess and she still figures quite prominently into Shinto religion and the Japanese culture. She has a very special relationship to royalty in Japan because:**

1. She makes the dreams of princes come true
2. She is prayed to in the Japanese tea ceremony
3. The older Japanese ladies keep her alive
4. All Japanese Emperors are believed to be of a lineage that originates from her

E. **Most ancient cultures had temple priestesses who would initiate men to the goddess through lovemaking. This was a fully accepted rite of passage. Who was the ancient Sumerian goddess they worshipped?**

1. Innana
2. Aphrodite

3. Venus
4. All of the above

F **As legend has it, Hawaii's Pele is a fiery, passionate and angry goddess. She is mad because:**

1. She doesn't get to spew as much lava as she'd like
2. Her sister had an affair with her husband
3. She is a PMS goddess
4. All those annoying tourists

G. **Kali, the Hindu Mother goddess of destruction, transformation, and regeneration looks a little scary at first glance. She's pictured with skin that is black or blue, her tongue hanging wildly from her mouth. She carries weapons in her four arms, and a garland of men's heads hangs around her neck. She holds one (recently lopped off) head in her hand. Why is she so intense?**

1. She doesn't like men
2. It's her role to go into the darkness, slay the ego and take in our sins
3. The Hindu tradition doesn't like beautiful goddesses
4. She represents women's sins

H. **In Hinduism, it is believed the Gods cannot exist without the powers of the goddesses. Divine feminine energy has a sacred name. What is it called?**

1. Radha
2. Shatki
3. Ganga
4. Gauri

I. **Shamanic cultures have long honored the divine feminine as "Mother," the earth herself. By what name is she known** by Peruvian shamans?

1. Woman who is Earth
2. Earth Mother
3. Green Woman
4. Pachamama

J. Native American cultures honor all creatures as Earth's children. There is one four-legged that is especially sacred, as its hardness and softness represent The Mother. Which sacred creature is considered symbolic of the goddess?

1. Turtle
2. Deer
3. Beaver
4. Mama Bear

K. Using tiny boats launched from the shores, Brazilian women make offerings of food and flowers to a beloved Yoruban ocean goddess, whom they credit with helping them heal their lives. By what name is she known?

1. Oshun
2. Chang-O
3. Oysa
4. Yemaya

L. Maeve is a powerful Celtic goddess whose legend was transformed in order to keep her alive in the Christian culture. Although the ancients considered her a goddess, as her story evolved she was referred to as a:

1. Princess
2. Mother of a King
3. Queen
4. Consort to Merlin

M. Long before the image of Mary with baby Jesus pervaded many cultures, there was a world-famous Mother goddess who was often pictured holding and nurturing her infant son. What was the name of this mother and son once worshipped in Egypt?

1. Isis and Horus
2. Nefethys and Anubis
3. Aphrodite and Cupid
4. Venus and Eros

N. Ancient Egyptians believed a host of deities would judge their worth in the afterlife. The Goddess of Truth and Justice would weigh the heart of the deceased. If it were light as a feather, he or she would go on; if the heart was heavy and laden with bad deeds, it would be tossed and the soul's journey would end. What is the name of this Egyptian Goddess of Justice and Right Order?

1. Libra
2. Osiris
3. Thoth
4. Maat

O. Sekhmet, the powerful Egyptian Goddess of War has a female body and an animal's head. What animal is she?

1. Cow
2. Tiger
3. Pussycat
4. Lion

CORRECT ANSWERS TO QUIZ

A. 1 Venus
B. 4. Pomegranate
C. 1. Vessel to hold and pour the tears of the world.
D. 4. All Japanese Emperors are believed to be of a lineage that originates from her
E. 4. Innana
F. 2. Her sister had an affair with her husband
G. 2. It's her role to go into the darkness, slay the ego and take in our sins
H. 2. Shatki
I. 4 Pachamama
J. 1. Turtle
K. 4. Yemaya
L. 3. Queen
M. 1. Isis and Horus
N. 4. Maat
O. 4. Lion

RATE YOURSELF!

- If you got one to five answers right, study up a little more
- If you got six to 12 answers right, you are on your way to goddess awareness
- If you got 13 to 20 answers right, you rock the goddess

My Journey

SEARCHING FOR THE DIVINE FEMININE BETWEEN THE LINES

THE PATH TO THE GODDESS *is not always easy. It is not carved out for you in our modern world. I share with you my journey to embracing the feminine divine. I wrote this in 1998. It was the first talk I was asked to give about The Goddess, at a Sunday morning service at an interfaith church in New York City. This was the beginning of my adventures with the Goddess. May it help you with yours.*

I always had a sense that if there was a God, there had to be a Goddess. *Host-Hostess. Steward-Stewardess. Actor-Actress.* In my heart, I think I knew there had to be a yin to the yang I grew up knowing as the Divine source of all that is. I just did not have a clue as to how to find Her.

It wasn't until I was in seminary school that I began to truly see the many feminine faces of God, known as Goddess, as she exists in so many of the world's religions and traditions. My path included many bumps, questions, and doubts along the way. I share my insights with you because I suspect that many people raised in our traditional religious culture may find it hard to believe—and perhaps even sacrilegious to consider—that the male God of the Bible is one of many interpretations of divine presence that exist in the world's religions.

Fortunately, I was trained by a seminary that encourages

free thinking and exploration. Its motto is "Never instead of, always in addition to." In order to embrace all faiths, we were taught that God is one source and yet that source manifests in many ways, through many paths, religions, and spiritual practices. And that God is represented by a wide range of deities with different names.

Nevertheless, the fear of acknowledging a feminine face of God grabbed hold of me in the middle of seminary school. I was doing what seminarians are supposed to do ... *grappling with God*. As I studied comparative religion, I was trying to reconcile the belief system I was raised with—*God is a man, no two ways about it*—with the new belief systems I was learning: *The Divine is neither male or female and/or The Divine is indeed both male and female*. One day I was praying to a feminine deity and I became panic-stricken: What if the male God gets mad at me and cuts me off? What if he's saying, *Oh, switching teams, eh? We'll see about that ...*

Many people are even afraid to consider the Divine as feminine in form or nature. Yet I learned on my personal journey that in order to be truly whole, whether we are women or men, we must embrace both the male and feminine aspects of the divine—and we must embrace those aspects of ourselves and of one another.

I discovered that I am among so many women—and men—searching for spirituality that brings both The Father and The Mother to the table. As we desperately seek balance and peace on our planet, and in these times of deeply disturbing and frightening world events, many of us are searching for what's been missing in modern life. And I believe one of the most important missing pieces of our lives has been The Sacred Feminine—not instead of, but *in addition to*, The Sacred Male. In the tradition of all-inclusive spirituality, we refer to the Divine as God, Goddess, All there is.

SHE IS THERE, IN BETWEEN THE LINES

When I first began to search for signs of the Mother in the world's religions, I found a few beautiful examples, including the "she aspect." One was in the gentle spiritual practice known as Taoism, founded by Loa Tzu in the 6th Century B.C.E.. The Taoists explain the origin of all that is as feminine, yet is manifested as both male and female, in what is known as the Yin and the Yang. It is this energy that the Taoist religious text *Tao Te Ching* attributes to the creation of the cosmos. "Conceived of as having no name, it is the originator of heaven and earth ... it is the Mother of all things."

In Kabbalah, the mystical aspect of Judaism, the indwelling aspect of God, also known as Shekhinah, is considered to be the feminine aspect of God. Kabbalists also know the soul as "She." Consider this petition to the divine from the tradition of mystical Judaism:

> *"My soul aches to receive your love. Only by the tenderness of your light can she be healed. Engage my soul that she may taste your ecstasy."*

The Judaic scriptures and the Gnostic Christian doctrines also include wisdom as a feminine aspect. She is called, Sophia and considered the personification of wisdom.

The Buddhists confer that Praj-na-para-mita (which means the perfection of wisdom) is feminine. An important Buddhist text, *Sariputra*, puts it this way: "*The perfection of wisdom gives light, O Lord. I pay homage to the perfection of wisdom. She is worthy of homage. She is unstained and the world cannot stain her.*"

Then of course, there is Grace. In Christian Theology it is the expression of God's love in his free and unmerited assistance. And, as the New Testament puts it, Grace can only be conferred through Faith. Isn't it interesting that those are names assigned to women? That Grace and Faith evoke perhaps the greatest sense of connection to the Divine, yet do so in the name and essence of the feminine. I was excited to see that when you dig around a bit you will find the feminine between the lines of well-established religions. Still, I was searching for a God who looked like me—feminine in nature and in her manifestations. The spiritual mother I longed for.

HAIL MARY

Conventional religious belief is obviously dominated by references to and images of a male Divine, whispering ever so softly of feminine energies between the lines. Yet Catholicism has given us our most tangible mainstream connection. Mary, mother of God's only begotten son, along with a handful of popular female saints, have been the most highly visible aspect of the feminine in the traditional religion for 2,000 years. Because of that, The Blessed Virgin cuts across religious boundaries. She is, in many ways, the adopted spiritual mother of all women, and people of many faiths embrace her. She has been solely responsible for keeping the sacred feminine alive for a couple of millennium. Yet there are many cultures that are rich with mythology, spiritual practices, religious experiences, and sacred texts that show us many ways in which The Goddess has been and can be worshipped, remembered and evoked.

It is extraordinary to realize that just over 2,000 years ago, *less than forty years before the birth of Jesus Christ*, queen Cleopatra of Egypt prayed to the mother goddess, Isis, who was the favored deity of the Queen's temples. Cleopatra's beloved, Julius Caesar, bowed to Isis' Roman counterpart, the goddess Venus. What was considered sacrilegious in their day was not the worship of goddesses ... but Caesar's worship of Cleopatra, which was so intense that he erected a statue of Cleopatra as Venus, but looking like Isis, in a holy temple to the Roman goddess. The Romans did not appreciate *that* interfaith approach to goddess worship back then.

When the Romans conquered Egypt, they ultimately replaced the antiquities and images of Isis and her infant Horus with images and icons of Mary and the baby Jesus.

Although Mary and Jesus are the most famous mother and child, the image of the mother and the child (or the pregnant, fertile mother) abound as a motif of cultures that worshiped The Great Mother. Joseph Campbell often said that the same essence of the Divine Feminine could be found in the religious mythology and folklore of every culture. Many of the stories are the same, yet the names and specific circumstances change according to cultural tradition.

HISTORY OF THE GODDESS

The earliest signs of goddess worship date as far back as 35,000 years ago. One of the most famous artifacts of the Divine Feminine is The Venus of Willendorf, which is believed to have been carved in stone 20,000 to 30,000 thousand years ago. And while she looks like a rotund female—pregnant and voluptuous—when you place a replica of her famous statue flat on her back, she takes on the form of the earth, the hills and valleys, mountains and ravines, are all in her body.

And that is how the ancients worshiped The Great Mother—as Mother of the Earth, Mother Earth and Mom Nature. They followed an earth-based religion. The Great Goddess Mother was the earth—alive, growing, pulsating with life. She was fertility, death, and regeneration, as witnessed in the flowers and trees, the moon, and the ocean, the cycles of life and nature. She was seen in so many diverse forms—fluid, capable of assuming any role. Much like our own mothers.

She was revered as the great power because women were seen as the great power. It was human women who could conceive, birth, and nurture children from their own bodies. A Miracle. But a miracle akin to the magic of Mother Earth—who could nurture flowers in the summer, protect them in her womb in the winter, and magically let them grow again in spring.

It is believed by many scholars that it was the eruption of violence as perpetrated by the newer, male-dominated cultures that obliterated the peaceful, earth-honoring ways of Goddess worship and paved the way for the stronghold of Christianity and eventually the obliteration of the Goddess from religion, religious texts, and teachings.

NATIVE AMERICAN AND INDIGENOUS SHAMANIC CULTURES

The shamanic religion—50,000 years old and still going strong, and considered the oldest of all religions—also reveres the mother, along with the father. She is the earth, the Great Mother. Some cultures call her Pachamama or Corn Woman. She is the nurturer who feeds us from her own body and sustains all of life. In Native American cultures, she is represented by the turtle—a hard shell with a soft inside. A popular Lakota chant sums it up well: *The earth is our mother ... we must take care of her.*

WHO IS THE GODDESS?

Like most people who are unfamiliar with the concept and rich spirituality of including The Goddess, the first time I began to explore the aspect of Feminine Divine called Goddess I was afraid that it meant I had to worship only a SHE and practice a spirituality that excluded men. Wrong.

Almost three decades ago, Merlin Stone wrote a groundbreaking book called *When God Was A Woman*, tracing cultures that worshipped "The Goddess" or "Goddesses." She described Goddess this way: She is the "divine feminine principle" or the "sacred feminine principle in the universe."

In this millennium we are seeing a resurgence of the Divine

Feminine and an observance of the feminine as sacred. We are seeing her in history, art, folklore, religion, spirituality, archeology, media, and mythology.

Many scholars and clergy agree that we need Her help to midwife this new point in history ... Because she brings to our world—and our lives—those qualities that, as discussed, even some traditional religions and most mystical religions assign as feminine qualities: Wisdom and the expression of the Soul. When we tap into wisdom and follow the call of our souls we can then forgive, be tolerant, appreciate everyone's individual evolution, and love without conditions. The energy of the Divine Feminine also balances the energy of the male; without it, the qualities traditionally associated with male energy—which include warring and aggression—will get completely out of hand.

RICH SPIRITUAL TRADITIONS AND RELIGIOUS MYTHOLOGY CAN HELP IN EVERYDAY LIFE

The natural progression of my search for the Divine Feminine is to write a book that puts together all that I have learned about the Goddess and how she can help us in our daily lives. In researching my book, *A Goddess Is A Girl's Best Friend* (published by Penguin in Fall 2002 and later republished by Llewellyn in 2008 as *The Goddess Pages, with an anniversary edition out in 2020*), I found thousands of ways the Divine Feminine is personified in different cultures. The rich mythology of the Feminine Divine has reemerged to offer role models—and guidance—to modern men and women. She comes to us as The Maiden, The Lover, The Mother, and also The Wise Woman. She is also Sister, Daughter, Best Friend. For example:

- The Greek goddess Aphrodite, also known as the Roman goddess Venus, is goddess of love and infatuation. She has completely insinuated herself in our culture, helping us to evoke the love within us all and encouraging us to experience high romance.

- The Egyptian goddess Isis is one of the most revered goddesses, worshipped as Queen of Heaven in the ancient Egyptian religions. A healing and resurrection goddess who was also considered a physician, she brought her beloved Osiris back to life from the dead and bore his child Horus, who went on to be the chosen son to represent the Father, on earth. She lives on through her image and energy in reliefs on ancient temples and tomb walls. She shows us we can heal, survive our grief, and live fruitful lives.
- The Chinese goddess Kuan Yin is a beautiful Bodhisattva who has captured the heart of
- Buddhist worshipers and beyond, just as Mary has captured the heart of so many in her religion of origin and around the world. She comes to tell us to be merciful and compassionate—especially to be our own merciful mothers.
- Lakshmi is the Hindu goddess of good fortune who brings abundance and beauty into our lives, pouring her gifts upon us. She, like Aphrodite, was born of the milky waters of the sea. She is symbolized as a beautiful woman with four arms, one pouring coins into the ocean from whence she came. She is still worshipped daily in Hindu temples and homes as are all goddesses in that tradition.

ALL THAT IS DIVINE IS BOTH FEMALE AND MALE

The Hindus teach us that the Divine essence of all that is, is the creative summary of both male and female principle. And so do the Taoists, who show us the feminine and the masculine principle that feed one another and make up the whole in the symbol of Yin/Yang. The circle of black and white halves show two opposite energies, from whose interactions and fluctuation, the universe, and its diverse forms emerge. Tibetan Buddhist do the same with their most sacred objects, dorje and bell. The bell represents the feminine and the dorje is the male principle. No worship service is ever conducted without use of each, together, one held in each hand.

In these systems of belief ... You can't have one without the other. You can't have day without the night. You can't have man without woman, or masculine without feminine. In very, very simple form, you can forget about toast for the rest of your life ... you can't plug in a toaster without both the male plug and the female outlet.

When we really understand that the Divine nature of all that is contains both the masculine and the feminine principles, it begins to make sense that men and women each contain those Divine principles; that the energy of the goddess exists within all of us; and that one energy might at some times be more prominent than the other. For example, any man or woman in a traffic jam may choose to evoke their male energy by vocalizing dissatisfaction with the traffic or even trying by driving aggressively. On the other end of the spectrum, both the man and the woman who share a moment of gentle nurturing and loving are operating from a more receptive and gentle feminine energy.

We are all children of God, Goddess, All There Is. When we acknowledge that we are all Divine, as well as complex beings that are both feminine and masculine in nature, we can begin to access true balance in our lives. It is in acknowledging that these qualities exist in all of us that we begin to find balance in our relationship to ourselves, our relationships to one another, and in our relationship to the world we live in.

Final Word

TOWARD BALANCE AND PEACE

"The Goddess does not rule the world; She is the world."
—Starhawk

TO TRULY CONNECT WITH THE Goddess, it helps to understand that she is part of our every day. She is the earth we stand on, and the elements of our common being. She is not separate from us. She is the one who gives life. It is to her we shall all return at the end of our days when our bodies become part of her body, or our ashes are scattered into the breath of her winds.

As we desperately seek balance and peace on our planet, and in these times of deeply disturbing and frightening world events, many of us are searching for what's been missing in modern life. Could it be we have been bereft of our spiritual link to the Sacred Feminine—not instead of, but *in addition to*, The Sacred Male? We are at a time in history where both women and men are crying out for their divine "Mother" and seeking a spirituality that brings both divine parents to the table, not just one, or the other.

The Divine Mother does not discriminate or love only those who worship in Her name. Her energy, presence, and possibility are available to anyone, of any religion, race, sex, gender-neutral sex, culture, background, and belief system.

One of the historical hallmarks of the Divine Mother is that by honoring ourselves, our earth and all living things, we honor Her. This kind of reverence does not need to be sorted into a religion or a particular belief system. It is more of a philosophy for living that can inspire us to a spiritual path of stability and peace.

I believe we must honor the feminine on all levels in our world—including our earth—in order to restore and heal our relationship to ourselves, to one another, and in the world we live in.

CHAPTER NOTES

Many sources of wisdom used are attributed within the pages of the lessons, and in the Bibliography. The following is list of attributions for the epigraphs at the start of each chapter and the prayers in Lesson Fourteen.

INTRODUCTION
Epigraph: Carol P. Christ
From: https://www.goddessariadne.org/why-women-need-the-goddess-part-1

LESSON ONE
Epigraph: Joseph Campbell
From: ***The Mythic Image*** (New Jersey: Princeton University Press, 1981)

LESSON TWO
Epigraph: Rhiannon Cameron
From: *Goddess Religion* © Rhiannon Cameron, 2000 – Used with permission

LESSON THREE
Epigraph: Laurie Sue Brockway
From: *The Goddess Pages* (Goddess Communications, 2020)

LESSON FOUR
Epigraph: Sharon Turnbull, Ph.D.
From: *Goddess Gift* (Quiet Time Press, 2007)

LESSON FIVE
Epigraph: Homer
From: *The Iliad* (Public Domain)

LESSON SIX
Epigraph: Miki Raver
From: *Listen to Her Voice* (San Francisco: Chronicle Books; First Edition, 1998)

LESSON SEVEN
Epigraph: Merlin Stone
From: *Ancient Mirrors of Womanhood, Volume II* (New York: New Sibylline Books, 1979)

LESSON EIGHT
Epigraph: Auntie Matter
From: "White Tara Invocation", www.whitetara.com/whitetara.html

LESSON NINE
Epigraph: D. Debroy
From: The Booklet ***Lakshmi Puja***

LESSON TEN
Epigraph: Athon Veggi and Alison Davidson
From: *The Book of Doors* (Rochester, Vermont: Destiny Books, 1994)

LESSON ELEVEN
Epigraph: Robert M. Pirsig
From: *Zen and the Art of Motorcycle Maintenance* (New York: HarperTorch; First Edition, 2006)

LESSON TWELVE
Epigraph: Zsuzsanna Budapest
From: "We All Come from the Goddess" – Song Lyric www.zbudapest.com

LESSON THIRTEEN
Epigraph: Starhawk
From: *The Spiral Dance: A Rebirth of the Ancient Religion of the Goddess* (New York: HarperOne; 20th Anniversary Edition, 1999)

LESSON FOURTEEN
Prayer: Connia Silver, © 1994, Used with permission

Prayer: Lisa Thiel
From: "Lady of the Lake" – Song Lyric from the album "Ladyslipper", © 1992, Used with permission

Prayer: Classic Hindu Prayer
From: Hindunet.com

Prayer: Sabbath Prayer to the Hebrew Goddess, Shekhina
From: *The New Synagogue Prayer Book* © Rabbi Joseph Gelberman/Rabbi Roger Ross

Prayer/Song: Zsuzsanna Budapest
From: "We All Come from the Goddess" – Song Lyric www.zbudapest.com

Prayer/Song: Classic Chants (Unknown and Lakota)

Prayer: Miriam Therese Winter
From: *Life Prayers* (New York: HarperCollins, 1998)

Prayers by Laurie Sue Brockway appear in *The Goddess Pages*.

FINAL WORD

Epigraph: Starhawk
From: *The Spiral Dance: A Rebirth of the Ancient Religion of the Goddess* (New York: HarperOne; 20th Anniversary Edition, 1999)

BIBLIOGRAPHY

An Anthology of Sacred Texts By & About Women, edited by Serenity Young (Crossroad Press, 1993)

Encyclopedia of GODS: Over 2,500 Deities of the World, by Michael Jordon (Facts on File, 1993)

Holy Bible (St. James)
Hymn for the Sabbath Eve (Friday Sundown), by Rabbi Isaac Luria, the Ari Zaal (Safed Spirituality, Lawrence Fine, Translator, Paulist Press, 1984)

Kabbalah As I See It, by Rabbi Joseph H. Gelberman (self-published). Rabbi Gelberman, founder of the New Seminary, is credited with having coined the phrase: "Never instead of, always in addition to."

Lakshmi Magic, By Laurie Sue Brockway (Goddess Communications,2015)

Listen To Her: Women of The Hebrew Bible, by Miki Raver (Chronicle Books, 1998)

Men and the Goddesses: Feminine Archetypes in Western Literature, by Tom Absher (Park Street Press, 1990)

Return of The Great Goddess, edited by Burleigh Muten (Stewart, Tabori & Chang, 1997)

The Charge of the Goddess - The Poetry of Doreen Valiente, Doreen Valiente (Centre For Pagan Studies Ltd, 2014).

The Devi Gita: The Song of the Goddess, Translation, Annotation, Commentary by C. Mackenzie Brown (SUNY Press, 1998)

The Goddesses In Art, by Lanier Graham (Artebras, 1997)

The Goddess Pages, by Laurie Sue Brockway, (Llewellyn, 2008)

The Goddess Sekhmet: The Way of The Five Bodies, by Robert Masters. (Amity House, 1988)

The New Book of Goddesses and Heroines, by Patricia Monaghan (Llewellyn Publications, 1997)

The Oxford Dictionary of World Religions, edited by John Bowker (Oxford Press, 1997)

When God Was A Woman, by Merlin Stone (Hartcourt-Brace, 1976)

When The Drummers Were Women, by Layne Redmond (Three Rivers Press, 1998)

365 Goddesses: A Daily Guide to the Magic and Inspiration of the Goddess, by Patricia Telesco
(HarperOne, 2010)

PHOTO CREDITS

Cover Design and Interior Formatting by Qamber Designs & Media
Images used under license from Shutterstock.com
and DepositPhotos.com

Cover Image and Lesson Eight: **Buddhist Goddess White Tara**
Lekhra/Depositphotos.com

Lesson One: **Nature Goddess, Rebirth**
Alex Tooth/Shutterstock.com

Lesson Two: **Venus of Willendorf**
Mountainpix/Depositphotos.com

Lesson Three: **African Woman**
Nejron Photo/Shutterstock.com

Lesson Four: **Spiral Goddess**
Tata Donets/Shutterstock.com

Lesson Five: **Artistic Woman Portrait**
Coka/Shutterstock.com

Lesson Six: **Fantasy Woman Sensation**
Cokacoka/Shutterstock.com

Lesson Seven: **Luminous Goddess of Light and Life**
Jozef Klopacka/Shutterstock.com

Lesson Nine: **Goddess Lakshmi**
sahuad/Depositphotos.com

Lesson Ten: **Egyptian Lion Goddess Sekhmet**
Izanbar/Depositphotos.com

Lesson Eleven: **Hindu Goddess Kali**
Mazeina/Depositphotos.com

Lesson Twelve: **Goddess as Protective Spirit on Earth**
JozefKlopacka/Depositphotos.com

ABOUT THE AUTHOR

Rev. Laurie Sue Brockway has written extensively on women's spirituality, self-esteem, emotional health, relationships, and weddings.

Her deep interest in Goddess studies began when she was a journalist specializing in women's empowerment, and it led her to become an ordained minister focused on interfaith spirituality and women's spirituality. The foundation of her ministry is to celebrate all traditions and to include all aspects of the Divine.

For more than 20 years Rev. Laurie Sue has presided over a multicultural wedding ministry based in New York and is widely recognized as an expert on interfaith, intercultural, and highly personalized nondenominational weddings. She has been called upon by couples around the world for her assistance in complex spiritual and cultural issues, and to help guide families through the interfaith marriage process. She honors relationships between all couples and believes in focusing on the common denominator of love.

Rev. Laurie Sue is author of many books, has written articles for hundreds of publications, and has been editor-in-chief of two national magazines. She also served as a senior editor at *Beliefnet* and *Everyday Health* and as a relationship columnist for *Huffpost.*

She is a graduate of the New Seminary for Interfaith Studies. She received her B.A. in Human Development from S.U.N.Y and studied Marriage and Family Therapy at Mercy College.

OTHER BOOKS BY THIS AUTHOR

Lakshmi Magic
The Goddess Pages
Wedding Goddess
Your Interfaith Wedding
Your Hindu-Interfaith Ceremony
Your Perfect Wedding Vows
Your Unique Ceremony
Pet Prayers and Blessings

Visit Rev. Laurie Sue at:
www.RevLaurieSue.com

If You Are Interested in the Divine Feminine You'll Love

THE GODDESS PAGES

By Laurie Sue Brockway

Every woman could use a bit of Goddess wisdom in her life.

Do you want to explore your personal power and claim your passions? Do you seek advancement in your career? Are you searching for love, or trying to get free of a bad romance? Do you wish you had more confidence and courage? The Divine Feminine is here to help you achieve the love, success, and happiness that you deserve.

Get ready to feel empowered: you are about to meet thirty-six of the most revered spiritual heroines from faiths and traditions around the world. Use this book to call upon each one for support, guidance, and inspiration in all areas of your life. Evoke their unique energies and strengths through rituals, meditations, gatherings, prayers, blessings, and many more fun and creative activities.

- Celebrate your true beauty with Hathor
- Unleash your dark and wild side with Lilith
- Free yourself from unhealthy relationships with Persephone
- Take aim at your career goals with Artemis
- Own and explore your sensuality with Oshun
- Find protection and healing with Tara
- Manifest spiritual and material wealth with Lakshmi

The Goddess Pages is a unique and empowering book that helps you connect with the strength and beauty of the Goddess–and experience the divine within you.

LAKSHMI MAGIC

We can all use more money, great job opportunities, and goodness in life. This book tells you how to invite material and spiritual wealth on all levels. And it gives you dozens of rituals, prayers, and techniques to draw prosperity and beauty into your life with the help of Goddess Lakshmi. Lakshmi, the Hindu Goddess of Good Fortune, has been bringing good things to life for five thousand years.

In this small but powerful book, the author reveals the spiritual secrets she learned and adapted during many years of study. The writing is fun and easy to follow. You will discover:

- The mythology and meaning of Lakshmi
- How to invite her grace into your life
- Rituals and devotions to attract Lakshmi's attention

- Prayers to ask for her blessings
- Insights into traditional Hindu worship
- Ideas for inviting good fortune into your life
- Peace of mind in times of financial struggle

Lakshmi is famous and beloved for her awesome role of bringing prosperity, opportunity, and success into your life.

GODDESS COMMUNICATIONS,
LLC NEW YORK

Made in the USA
Las Vegas, NV
02 August 2024